J92   AC 41874 ✓
JACKSON
Hilton, Suzanne

The World of Young Andrew Jackson

D1446846

The World
of Young
Andrew Jackson

Historical books
by Suzanne Hilton

The World of Young Herbert Hoover
The World of Young George Washington
The World of Young Tom Jefferson
We the People: The Way We Were, 1783–1793
Faster than a Horse: Moving West with Engine Power
Getting There—Frontier Travel without Power
The Way It Was—1876

The World
of Young
Andrew Jackson

Suzanne Hilton

illustrated by Patricia Lynn

J92
puch
Replacement
ISBN 0- 8027 - 6814 - 8
LC 88-5783

Walker and Company
New York

First published in the United States of America
in 1988 by the Walker Publishing Company, Inc.

Published simultaneously in Canada by Thomas Allen & Son
Canada, Limited, Markham, Ontario.

Library of Congress Cataloging-in-Publication Data
Hilton, Suzanne.
   The world of young Andrew Jackson / Suzanne Hilton ;
illustrated by Patricia M. Lynn.
     p. cm.
   Bibliography: p.
   Includes index.
   Summary: Focuses on the early years of the skinny red-
head who became America's first backwoods president.
   ISBN 0-8027-6814-8.   ISBN 0-8027-6815-6 (lib. bdg.)
   1. Jackson, Andrew, 1767–1845—Childhood and
youth—Juvenile literature.   2. Presidents—United States—
Biography—Juvenile literature.   [1. Jackson, Andrew,
1767–1845—Childhood and youth.   2. Presidents.]   I.
Lynn, Patricia M., ill.   II. Title.
E382.H55   1988
973.5'6'0924—dc19
[B]   88-5783
[92]   CIP
                                                             AC

Printed in the United States of America
10 9 8 7 6 5 4 3 2 1

Contents

Author's Note

WHY A BOOK ABOUT
ONLY THE EARLY YEARS?

No person, even a general or president of the United States, can grow up without having some sort of childhood. The body grows more mature, the hair on top may thin or turn gray, and the brain grows wiser. But the child is always inside the adult.

Many fine books have been written about Andrew Jackson. But the most important years of his life are usually skipped over in a few pages.

Andrew Jackson's childhood experiences made him the kind of man that he was. I set out to learn more about those early adventures—the part he played in the American Revolution, the neighborhood he lived in, the mistakes he made, the family he lost, and the friends he found.

Where does such new information come from? Often from the diaries of eyewitnesses who lived in the same time and place as Jackson. The description of Charleston, South Carolina, its firefighters, homes, gardens, streets, and plantation life, came from the diary of a young man who was able to put into words the sights that young Andrew saw the same year. Court cases and names of people who went to court when Andrew was a beginning lawyer appear in the diary of Spruce Macay, Andrew's first law teacher in Salisbury, North Carolina. How Andrew chose a good horse is told in a 1780s book on farriery and horseracing. What Andrew learned about dueling is in a 1790s book for young men who wanted to know the rules of dueling.

Andrew Jackson did not grow up gently. He took many wrong turns, but he learned from his mistakes. When he was a general, his soldiers worshiped him. His political enemies said he was a ruffian and a murderer. He was the first president of the United States who had not been raised and educated as a "gentleman."

Andy, the fiery tempered child who grew up in the Waxhaw region of South Carolina, was inside "Old Hickory" all the time.

—Suzanne Hilton

Acknowledgments

The author wishes to acknowledge the generous and professional help given by The Library Company of Philadelphia; the Lancaster County Library of Lancaster, South Carolina; the North Carolina State Archives in Raleigh, North Carolina; the Historical Society of Pennsylvania in Philadelphia; the Andrew Jackson State Park; the Family History Department of the Genealogical Library in Salt Lake City, Utah; and the Jenkintown Library of Jenkintown, Pennsylvania.

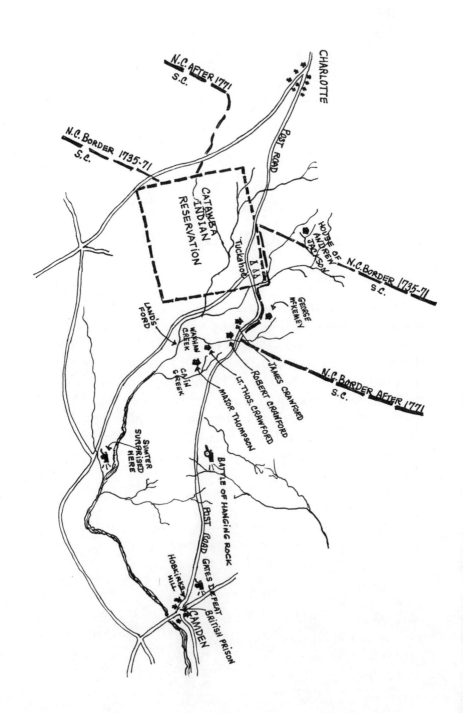

CHARLOTTE

N.C. AFTER 1771
S.C.

N.C. BORDER 1735-71
S.C.

POST ROAD

CATAWBA INDIAN RESERVATION

HOUSE OF ANDREW JACKSON

N.C. BORDER 1735-71
S.C.

Tuckahoe

GEORGE McKEMEY

LAND'S FORD

WAXHAW CREEK

CAIN CREEK

ROBERT CRAWFORD

JAMES CRAWFORD

Lt. THOS. CRAWFORD

MAJOR THOMPSON

N.C. BORDER AFTER 1771
S.C.

SUMTER SURPRISED HERE

BATTLE OF HANGING ROCK

POST ROAD

HOBKIRK'S HILL

GATES DEFEAT

CAMDEN

BRITISH PRISON

1

The Saining

WHEN THEIR BROTHER was born on March 15, 1767, Hugh and Robert Jackson saw only a small rolled blanket with a bright red face topped by fuzzy red hair. The babe lay safely within the protecting half circle of Betty Jackson's arm. Then Aunt Margaret McKemey shooed them out of the room.

Rob and Hugh knew better than to ask the name of their new baby brother. Their mother would keep that a secret until the very moment he was baptized in the Waxhaw Presbyterian Church. If the fairies learned the baby's name, they might try to steal him. The boys had just gone to a funeral and seen the body of a baby stolen by the fairies while it was asleep.

Aunt Margaret insisted on having a saining, even though Betty Jackson herself was too exhausted to care. A saining was a blessing to protect a newborn child from the fairies until it could be baptized. Back in the old world the ancient Scottish custom had seemed right, but in the new world many people no longer believed in bad fairies.

"We'll take no chances," Margaret had told her sister Jennet. They both knew Betty had had bad luck aplenty so far in this new year. Jennet Crawford brought a fir candle and the Bible into the bedroom.

If only her husband Andrew had lived a few weeks longer, Betty thought. How proud he would have been to have another son. The small babe was already beginning to fill the emptiness that Andrew's death had left in her heart.

Margaret placed the family Bible on the bed and tucked a roll filled with cheese under Betty's pillow. Fairies could often be tempted by offerings of food and made to forget why they had entered the house of a newborn babe. Jennet lit the fir candle and carried it three times around the bed, reciting an ancient Scottish blessing to keep the mother and babe safe from harm. Then she placed the candle near the head of the bed.

The flickering candlelight only reminded Betty of the death candle she had lit for her young husband two weeks before. As she drifted in and out of sleep, her mind wandered back to happier days when they had left Ireland two years earlier.

She remembered especially one bitter cold night when the Irish winter's icy blast had turned the trees of Larne, County Antrim, into creaking demons and the soil underfoot into solid rock. Hugh Jackson, her husband's brother and late of His Majesty's Forty-Ninth Regiment of Foot, was telling them about the new provinces across the ocean.

If ever a man had a golden tongue and a way with words, it was that Hugh Jackson. He even made the savages sound like friends when he spoke of the Catawba Indians who had acted as guides for the soldiers. But it was when he spoke of food that a man could get for himself that the Jacksons listened seriously. Rivers filled with fish, and wild animals just for the taking!

The Jacksons and their neighbors had all known hunger. Many a dark night they had lured small animals or pheasants through the hedgerow and into their own yards. They planted parsley or an innocent-looking garden of pinks just to attract a hare. Sometimes they let the children drop a trail of seeds from the roadway into the yard in the hopes that a tasty pheasant might follow.

But the risk was great. If the lord of the manor ever caught them eating a fish from his brook or a bird from his land, he could send them to prison!

Before Hugh had left the Jackson's that night, he had talked seventeen of their neighbors—and himself—into sailing to the colonies in America to settle in what he called "the Garden of the Waxhaws" in Carolina. Already four of Betty Jackson's sisters lived there with their husbands. Margaret Hutchinson, the eldest, had married George McKemey. George was a kind man who had never learned to read and write. Jane Hutchinson, called Jennet, had gone to visit Margaret and married James Crawford. Jennet was not very strong, and she wrote home exciting letters about the large plantation they owned in the Waxhaws, where slaves did all the hard work and cared for their children. Mary and Sarah Hutchinson had sailed over more recently and found husbands.

An adventurous sparkle glowed in Betty's blue eyes when Andrew agreed to leave Ireland for the Carolinas. His father was a linen weaver and merchant in Carrickfergus. Business was good, but none of his sons wanted to become weavers. Betty spent the rest of the winter spinning heddie-yarn and weaving warm woolen clothes to take with them.

At the last minute before they left, Hugh's wife had hysterics. She flatly refused to leave Ireland and go where the Indians would likely have her scalp before she had unpacked her trunk. She frightened off most of the other families as well. But red-haired, spirited Betty Jackson was made of stronger material. She and Andrew packed up their sons, Hugh and Rob, and left Ireland in the spring of 1765.

The ocean voyage was much more uncomfortable than Mrs. Jackson had imagined, but she looked on it as a testing ground for the trials that would come when they settled in the wilderness. Surely, building a home of logs and clearing land where no man had ever farmed before was going to take strong men and women who could live a few years without all the comforts of home. In four weeks at sea, the passengers almost forgot what it was like to be well-fed and dry and to have their privacy. Somewhere a child was always sick, an old person dying, and a babe wailing.

The wailing of her own babe suddenly interrupted Betty's memories of happier times when her Andrew was beside her. For an instant she was startled, but she soon had her newborn son contented. Margaret and Jennet looked in on her, but went away quickly when they found the babe had quieted and Betty had closed her eyes. She was not ready to talk yet.

Betty had been silent too when the ship had dropped anchor and they had gone ashore. The Irish settlers had expected America to be very much like the mother country, but it was not. Here the children ran freely, shouting and laughing as they pleased. No one said, "Hush, you will disturb our neighbors," because, in the provinces, the houses were far apart.

Most of the houses were built of wood instead of stone, which seemed odd to the Jacksons. The stones, which would have been used to build houses at home, were piled up into fences here. Streets were straight lines instead of crooked lanes. Betty feared this new world must have a great many diseases. She knew that sickness came on the wind, although some folk believed it was brought only by witches. Back home the crooked, narrow streets were the very thing that kept the wind from blowing diseases from one home to another. Besides, here many houses had trees shading them from the sun. Betty knew for a fact that the sun must shine on the roof of a house to keep away sickness.

Outside the port city, the streets were either muddy or dusty, depending on the weather. The wagon wheels lumped up over tree roots, and bushes caught in the spokes. Andrew told Betty they had five hundred miles to travel to the Waxhaws.

No one knows where the Jacksons' ship landed, but it was probably in Philadelphia. They did not land in Charles Town (now called Charleston, South Carolina); we know that because their names are not listed on the port record of immigrants in that city.

The Jacksons probably visited relatives in southern Pennsylvania and then joined a large group of wagons traveling south along the Great Wagon Road. From Philadelphia to Lancaster, the road was very good. Andrew bought a strong small wagon and two oxen to pull it. Although some of the wagons were pulled by horses, friends warned them that they might have trouble finding food for the horses when they were farther south. Northern horses ate oats, but southern horses ate corn. Oats were hard to find in the south and cost as much as three pence for one sheaf. Oxen were much easier to feed.

Beyond Lancaster, the road went through York, Pennsylvania, and then dipped southwest toward where the Conococheague Creek emptied into the Potomac River. The Jacksons went to a place they called Caninigigo, Pennsylvania. Early biographers mistakenly guessed it to be Conowingo, near Baltimore. The people who lived near Conococheague, where the Great Wagon Road turned straight south, spelled the name "Canigogig" or "Canigochig." The Jacksons were most probably at the gathering place for immigrants who were taking the Great Wagon Road to the south, and not at Conowingo.

Most of their fellow travelers had lived in Pennsylvania awhile and were now heading for new lands to the south. They could not go west from Pennsylvania because King George of England had closed all the land north of the Ohio River to settlers.

The parade of wagons was long. The wagon families, except for the first in line, choked all day from the dust raised by those in front. But when other drivers helped Andrew Jackson get his wagon through deep sticky mud or ford a stream that was deeper than expected, the Jacksons were glad for the company. Sometimes huge freight wagons, called "liners" and pulled by six or more horses, charged past the slow-moving parade. Drivers of liners were rude to those they called the "tramps," who shared their road.

Many days passed after the Jacksons saw the last bridge. After Conococheague, when they reached a stream too deep to ford, they had to pay for the ferry. Mr. Watkins owned

the ferry across the Potomac River, where Hagerstown, Maryland, is today.

The Great Wagon Road followed an old Indian trail down the long valley between the Blue Ridge Mountains and the "Devil's Backbone," a long high ridge on the eastern side of the Allegheny Mountains. The Alleghenies were the highest mountains that most of the immigrants had ever seen. Another ferry, owned by Mr. Ingles, carried the wagoners across the New River, where Roanoke, Virginia, is now. Some days later, the slow, dusty procession forded the Yadkin River in North Carolina. Then the road branched into several Indian trails. Often the wagon drivers had to pull over to make room for herds of cattle being driven to northern markets. A man who lived along the road said he counted over one thousand wagons traveling south the year of the Jacksons' journey.

Betty and the boys enjoyed waving to people in the smaller two-wheeled carts that passed by. They felt sorry for the travelers who had to sleep in the ugly log ordinaries and public houses. At an ordinary, each guest paid six pence for a warm meal of bacon, eggs, and hoecake and another six pence for a bed that he shared with a stranger. Besides being narrow and already occupied by fleas and bedbugs, the bed had only one brown sheet. On a cold night, a man used his greatcoat for a blanket. He paid six pence for his horse to spend the night in a pasture, and more for the horse in a stable.

For the high price of sleeping one person at a tavern for one night, the Jacksons could buy Andrew a new pair of work shoes or an acre of land! They were glad they could sleep in their wagon.

2

A Winter Burying

WITH ALL THEIR possessions and supplies packed in, only a small space in the wagon was left for the family. But Betty Jackson had made it as cozy as possible, with quilts and blankets for Hugh and Rob to bounce on.

The oxen pulled the wagon so slowly that Andrew and the boys could get out and walk beside it while Betty handled the reins. All the wagons stopped for nooning, so the travelers could cook and eat the big meal of the day together. Someone kindled a large fire, and the women cooked for their own families, sharing gossip and chatter. Few of the travelers along the Great Wagon Road were heading for a special place, as the Jacksons were. Most were going to turn west near the town of Salisbury, North Carolina, and head beyond the Allegheny Mountains into new land they called "Caintuck," although some said the name was really "Kentucky." The King had also forbidden settlers to go there, but the general attitude was "I don't guess the King will follow us there!"

The wives were more worried about Indians than about the King's men.

"The Indian Wars have been over for four years," their husbands told them. "Treaties have been signed now, and there will be no trouble from Indians." A treaty-signing had always ended wars back in the old world. The settlers had no way of knowing that Indian wars did not end so simply in the new world.

Wives from the other wagons listened to Betty Jackson with envy when she told them that her family was heading for a place called the Garden of the Waxhaws, and that she already had four sisters waiting there to greet them.

Mrs. Jackson was not quite so confident, however, when they lumbered into Salisbury, in North Carolina province. Ten years before, this town had consisted of seven log cabins. Now it had sixteen public houses and several shops. The townspeople pointed proudly to their new courthouse built of logs.

After goodbyes to the settlers turning west, Andrew Jackson asked where to find the road toward the Waxhaws.

"Catawba Path heads that way," a townsman pointed, warning Jackson to keep their wagon on the dikes.

The main road turned west toward the mountains. The road the Jacksons followed was no more than an Indian trail, used occasionally by traders' wagons. It was so narrow in places that the wagon struck branches on both sides. Roots and small trees sometimes caught underneath. At other times the path ran along a sort of natural dike, with swamps on either side.

Often Andrew could not find a place wide enough for them to pull off and cook their supper or rest for the night. After dark, the howling wolves and an occasional screeching wildcat (or an Indian imitating a wild creature) kept the tired parents from the refreshing kind of deep sleep that Hugh and Rob enjoyed. Night and day they were tortured by small biting insects called "mosketoes," which seemed to be especially vicious the farther south they moved.

Rough wider trails sometimes crossed the path, but a trader on the road told them not to camp there because they were buffalo trails. No buffaloes had been seen lately, but you couldn't be too careful. If a herd decided to stampede, getting out of the way would be nearly impossible.

The fourth day after they left Salisbury, they came to Spratts—the last village that could be called a town before the Crawford plantation. Spratts had a log tavern, where court was held four times a year. A man told them that the town was plenty noisy and exciting at the public times when a traveling judge and lawyers came, but all was quiet and empty that night. A country store and a Presbyterian church were nearby at Sugar Creek. Betty Jackson counted about thirty buildings. To-morrow they would reach the Garden of the Waxhaws!

It was midsummer, and when the Jacksons finally rode into the Waxhaw region, a few wildflowers showed up against the lush green of the forest. But it was not the "Garden" they had dreamed of. The few houses they passed were built of rough unfinished logs. The people who watched suspiciously as their wagon rolled by looked unwashed and poor. Looking down at herself, Betty Jackson realized suddenly that her family looked even worse.

At last Jackson turned the wagon off the post road to a narrower one. The home of James and Jennet Crawford looked down on them from the top of a hill. In the first few minutes of greeting, all the discomforts of the journey were forgotten. They were home.

Andrew and Betty Jackson bought two hundred acres of land in Anson County from Thomas Ewing on Liggett's Branch. The branch was a stream of red water near the headwaters of Twelve-Mile Creek. Down that larger creek a man could float on a raft to the tumbling Catawba River, and even continue to the sea many miles farther south.

Their land was red clay rather than the rich bottom soil Andrew would have preferred, but this piece of land had some good points in its favor. It was only four miles from the post road used by the King's Post riders to carry mail and the news from the northern colonies to Charles Town in South Carolina province. Post roads were always kept in good repair by the King's command, so the Jacksons knew it would never be allowed to become overgrown.

Four miles down the post road, Betty Jackson's sister Margaret McKemey lived, and just beyond lived her sister Jennet. The other two sisters lived a day's journey away. The sisters were almost together again. But the deciding factor in buying the land was that Andrew Jackson could not pay for it all at once, and this was land that Thomas Ewing evidently agreed to let him pay for a little at a time.

In the spring of 1766 the surveyors arrived and measured the boundaries of the Jackson land from a white oak south of the creek to a red oak. They told Andrew that his land was not in Anson County, but in Mecklenburg County, province of North Carolina.

The first summer Andrew and Betty Jackson were able to plant only a small crop. The young parents planned to grow vegetable gardens and an orchard and to build a barn. But all that would take two or three years. Their small cabin was never completely finished.

Before the end of the second summer, Betty Jackson knew they would have a new baby in March. Her husband had begun clearing out trees and roots to make a field large enough to plant a corn crop. But now Betty could not help with the heavy work. Andrew never mentioned to her the pains that he felt when he lifted heavy logs.

One snowy February day Andrew had struggled hard to move an especially heavy tree root. Suddenly he doubled over in agony. Betty heard him cry out. She ran outside and managed to get him into the cabin, near the fireplace. But there was no doctor nearby to tell her what to do. A fierce storm raged outside. Andrew died the next morning before anyone could help.

The neighbors rode over as soon as they learned of the tragedy, and helped Mrs. Jackson ready her husband's body for the grave. The night was freezing cold, but after someone died, all the windows had to be opened wide. Betty's only mirror must be covered in black, and the clock they had brought all the way from Ireland stopped. The silence in the house made Betty feel they were all in a tomb.

Next morning the mourners began to arrive. Betty Jackson

would never have believed that His Majesty King George could make his presence felt at her husband's small funeral, but he did. Until now she had not known why the people in the provinces had hated the Stamp Act so much. Now it invaded her home.

One of the items taxed was black mourning clothes. Rather than pay the tax, the neighbors refused to wear black. Instead, they wore a black ribbon or armband on their Sunday clothes. James Crawford told Mrs. Jackson she was not even to give funeral gifts of gloves and scarves to the pallbearers, because those items also were taxed.

All night the neighbors sat with Andrew Jackson's body to protect it from the hostile spirits that walked abroad at night. The mourners needed a large amount of strong drink to per-form this sad duty, as James Crawford discovered when they emptied one gallon after another of his homemade brew.

Next morning the funeral procession began, with Betty and her children riding ahead in an open wagon. The pallbearers followed very slowly behind a mule that pulled the coffin on a sled through the snow and ice. The coffin had been used for many funerals, and was to be used many more times. The mourners stopped at the McKemey house along the way for more strong drink.

One of the pallbearers later told his grandson they had so much to drink that they had a great deal of trouble slipping about on an icy stretch near a creek. As they struggled uphill, no one noticed the body fall out through the hinged trap door at the foot of the wooden box.

They did not discover their loss until they reached the burying ground and found the box was empty. Embarrassed into a more sober state, the pallbearers·hurried back to find that the body had caught on some bushes at the bottom of the hill.

Meanwhile, James Crawford had sent out men to invite everyone to the funeral, and no one ever refused an invitation to a funeral. Now the crowd that waited for the body to be found was large and very cold. They soon drank up the rest of Crawford's homemade corn whiskey.

Two weeks after Andrew Jackson was buried, his son was born.

3

Cow Heaven Ways

FIVE WAGONLOADS of relatives flooded the small Waxhaw Presbyterian Church on the day the youngest Jackson was to be baptized.

Since it was also the first Sunday in the quarter, the church was overflowing with worshippers. Old practices die slowly, and the older farmers were in the habit of attending church services regularly—once every three months.

Although they would not admit it, even to each other, they came to church to preserve their cows from pranks played by disgruntled fairies. Unbaptized babies weren't the only ones in danger from fairies. All Scotch-Irish people knew that fairies moved to new underground homes every three months. Searching for a new home in another grassy hillock often made a bad fairy angry enough to dry up a family cow, especially if some unlucky farmer should plow a furrow through a fairy's new home. Many farmers still followed the old custom of letting one tree stand for a "fairy fort" in the center of their fields after the rest of the land had been cleared, so there would be no danger of such an accident.

The Reverend William Richardson beamed down on the large congregation from his high pulpit. He had prepared a fire-and-brimstone sermon that he delivered without reading.

When it came time for the baptism, Betty Jackson handed him a piece of paper with the baby's name written on it.

"Andrew Jackson," the preacher spoke the name aloud for the first time. But by then it was safe. Everyone smiled when the baby cried lustily, drowning out the rest of the Reverend Richardson's words. Since it was bad luck for babies not to cry when they were baptized, fathers sometimes handled their children roughly or mothers gave a little pinch through the blanket to assure good luck.

Betty Jackson's sisters, their husbands, and many children returned after the baptism to the Crawford plantation for a large celebration. The sisters had stood beside each other in the old world, and in the new, they often supplied their Waxhaw neighbors with topics for gossip.

One of the many Mrs. Samuel Dunlaps reported after a church service that Betty Jackson had now moved in with the Crawford family to stay. So many of the Dunlaps were christened Samuel that they were known by special names, like "River Samuel" who lived on the Catawba, and "South Samuel" who lived south of the church.

With three Jackson children and eight of the Crawfords, the log house was overflowing. But Jennet was almost an invalid. She needed her widowed sister's help almost as much as Betty needed a place to raise her sons. Betty brightened at the thought of being nearer to the church and her new Waxhaw friends.

Of all her new friends, Nancy Richardson was the favorite. Both Nancy and her husband were to play important roles in bringing up young Andrew Jackson.

Marrying Nancy had been one of the Reverend William Richardson's greatest accomplishments. Like many younger sons, he had had to make his own way in the world. According to English law, when a father died, he had to leave all the money and the family home to the eldest son, no matter how unworthy that son might be. Richardson's father had left their family home in England to his wild, drunken, and extravagant eldest son. William had managed to get his education in Scotland and then had sailed to Virginia to be a Presbyterian preacher.

He rode into the western mountains to be a missionary to the Cherokee Indians, but without success. On the way to Cherokee country, young Richardson preached at the Waxhaw church, where people asked him to stay. He married Nancy Craighead, the beautiful and spirited daughter of the well-known Reverend Alexander Craighead of Sugar Creek Presbyterian Church. Many of the strict church people found Nancy a little too spirited, with some high-minded ideas above the station of a preacher's wife. When William and Nancy had no children of their own, some of the nastier members of the congregation said that God must be punishing them.

Nancy Richardson loved children and was very unhappy about not having her own. One day William wrote to his sister's husband, Archibald Davie, to ask him to send over one of their sons so they could adopt him as their own. The boy, William Richardson Davie, was about six years old when he sailed from England in 1761 in the care of his older cousin, Robert Carr. Davie's parents arrived three years later, and they settled near the Waxhaw Church.

William Richardson Davie was twelve when Andrew Jackson was born, and one of the brightest boys Betty Jackson had ever met. He was taught by the Reverend Richardson. When the minister went off on one of his many preaching tours, Robert Carr saw to it that the boy never neglected his studies.

The surveyors who had measured the Jackson land now arrived at the Crawford and McKemey plantations. Their homes were in a stretch of land that had been measured incorrectly. For months, they and many of their neighbors were not sure whether they lived in North or South Carolina province.

Even the governor of North Carolina was embarrassed. He had built Fort Mill to protect the white settlers and friendly

Catawba Indians when the Cherokees went on the warpath. Now the governor learned he had built his fort, spending North Carolina money, in South Carolina by mistake!

The men of the Waxhaws grew hot and angry when they heard the boundary lines might be changed. A man was judged by what state he lived in, just as he had been back home in the old country. North Carolina people considered themselves much better than those who lived to the south of them. And South Carolina people pointed with pride to the culture and beauty of their large city of Charles Town, claiming that North Carolina did not even have a decent seaport.

Bands of "South Men" drove off new surveying parties and even the sheriff's posse from the north. Tempers became so hot that a company of militiamen came down the post road, the main road through the Waxhaws, and frightened off the unruly South Men. George McKemey and James Crawford were North Men, but when the land was surveyed again, McKemey discovered his home was four hundred yards inside North Carolina. The Crawford home, just a half mile away, was in South Carolina.

James Crawford, who had only bad things to say about the South Men, suddenly discovered that he was one of them. He had to go all the way to Charles Town to get a new deed to prove he owned his own land.

The squabble about which state their land was in would not have been important at all, except for the birth of Andrew Jackson, Jr. The Jackson home was always in North Carolina. But little Andrew was not born at home. To this day, no one knows for sure whether he was born at Aunt Margaret McKemey's in North Carolina, or at Aunt Jennet Crawford's in South Carolina.

Many years later, when he was asked where he was born, Jackson answered, "South Carolina is the state which gave me birth."

Social events in the Waxhaws were few. The most popular gatherings were cockfights, logrollings, vendues, and funerals.

Cockfights, between vicious trained cocks that had razor-sharp spurs attached to their legs, were for gamblers who bet on which cock would survive the bloody fight. Logrollings were wild contests to see who could keep his balance longest on a log afloat in the Catawba River. The men also bet on those.

The personal goods of someone who had recently died or who needed money in a hurry were sold at a vendue. There, a man or woman could buy something very valuable for a few pence—a book, a woolen jacket, a tool, a pair of spectacles. The prices at a vendue did not stay low very long, however, because the auctioneer brought out the whiskey jug, and the audience began bidding prices up much higher after that.

No person ever missed attending a funeral for fear people would not attend his. Two pallbearers carried the coffin, and two young boys were assigned the job of "underbearers." A black velvet pall, owned by the church, covered the coffin and also the heads and shoulders of the underbearers. Often the same coffin was used over and over. The body was released into its grave through the trap door at one end, and the coffin was saved for the next person who could not afford one of his own, or who died suddenly before a coffin could be made.

Each person in the funeral procession was assigned a place to walk and a companion to walk with, according to social rank. Conversation for days afterward centered on the gloomy event. Had the family served burnt wine, or just homemade whiskey? What was served at the meal afterward? And woe be to the family that did not give its deceased a proper sendoff as befit his station in life.

In the midst of these entertainments, the Reverend Richardson announced the first of his many "literary evenings." He had a large library of books, a real rarity in the South Carolina "upcountry," where most people could not read at all and most men signed their names with an X. The Hutchinson sisters were among the few women who could write and read. Living close to the Richardsons, on the Crawford plantation, Betty Jackson attended many literary evenings.

An idea began to grow in her mind. Young Hugh and Rob Jackson were true rough-and-tumble upcountry boys. They seemed made for the outdoor life. But the baby Andrew was still young enough to be molded. He could be a scholar—perhaps even a preacher.

Betty Jackson, a young woman in her thirties, was a bundle of energy. She had plenty of love to give all the Crawford children as well as her own. The Crawford girls were already married, except for Margaret. Margaret was probably an invalid, either physically or mentally. Expecting that she would never marry, her father made provisions for her to have a personal slave to care for her, and for her brother James to share his home with her as long as she lived. The older boys—James, Jr., Thomas, and Alexander—were starting to think of marriage. The two younger ones, Joseph and William, were closer to the ages of Rob and Hugh Jackson. Each year Jennet Crawford grew weaker and less able to care for her family.

Uncle James Crawford was no longer young. He was glad to have the young Jackson boys to help on the farm. When Hugh was seven years old, James told Betty Jackson it was time for him to be apprenticed.

Small fatherless boys and girls had to be taught a trade so they could support themselves. Girls were usually taught "housewifery" and were married off before they were eighteen. Boys learned their master's trade until they reached the age of twenty-one. An apprentice, no matter how young, left home and moved in with the master's family. An apprentice who ran away, boy or girl, was caught and punished. When a boy apprentice came of age, the master gave him two sets of clothing, one for church-going and one for everyday wear.

"You are indeed fortunate," James Crawford said to Hugh Jackson when the boy stood before him, fighting back the tears that stung his eyes and threatened to roll down his cheeks. Only girls cried, his mother had said sternly. "Many a grown man would give anything to live at the plantation of Squire Crawford and learn from him."

Squire Robert Crawford was the younger brother of Uncle James. His land began at the log fence back of James's cow pasture. He owned many more slaves and cattle than Uncle James, and a much larger house. The Squire and his wife had two little girls, so Hugh could understand why he needed a big boy of seven to help him.

Life on the Robert Crawford plantation would be a step up in the world for Hugh, Uncle James told him. The Squire was cultured and well-educated. Didn't the post rider sound his bugle at the Squire's house nearly every time he came down the post road, which was about every forty days? No one else in the Waxhaws received the newspapers from two large cities, when the King had forbidden newspapers to be delivered by mail. But it was not until Uncle James mentioned the cattle drives that he caught Hugh's complete attention.

At age seven, Hugh knew he wanted to become a cattle-driver more than anything else. Hadn't he pretended to be one of those expert horsemen every time he got on his pony? The cattledrivers, with a special outdoor odor on their clothing, were his heroes. Hugh had seen them drive Squire Crawford's cattle to the Cowpens to be fattened. And to the market twice a year—sometimes to Salisbury in North Carolina, but lately south to Charles Town, where the greatest sales were held.

"Cow Heaven" some of the settlers called the Waxhaws, because so many farmers had turned to cattle-raising. Hugh pictured himself riding behind the cattle, wielding a leather whip that cracked like the shot of a pistol. With a much lighter heart, he took leave of his mother, Rob, and Andy, and walked across the fields with his bundle of clothes.

With Hugh's future taken care of, Betty had more time to keep Rob at his chores and train Andy. Often in the evenings, James and Jennet discussed the plans they had for their own boys. As each Crawford son reached the age to marry, James sold him a large amount of land for five shillings.

Betty Jackson could do the same for her boys. But she would

not wait until they were older. James Crawford acted as witness to the deed that made the three little Jackson boys heirs to the land their father had bought on Liggett's Creek.

At the age of three, Andrew Jackson became a landowner.

4

Teachers and Rebels

A SNOWBALL FIGHT over a thousand miles away was to change Andy Jackson's life forever.

The snowballs, thrown in Boston on March 5, 1770, became rocks. Then the boys were replaced by angry men. What began with boys teasing the hated British soldiers turned into an ugly street fight. Two of the soldiers fired their guns into the crowd. They killed five men and wounded several others.

About five weeks later, Squire Crawford read the newspaper report of the incident to a large group gathered at the Waxhaw Church.

Betty Jackson heard the reading after church and told her sister and brother-in-law that it was called "the Boston Massacre." She tried to shrug off the cold fear that this was not just a small incident, soon to be forgotten in the pressures of everyday life. British soldiers firing on their own people! It was unthinkable.

The following Sunday, the crowd, waiting for the Squire to read more news from his newspapers, was nearly double in size. No longer was his audience content to hear just a portion of the news. They wanted to hear it all. But unless the post had come by, or someone had ridden into Charles Town that week, the Squire had no news to give them.

Squire Robert Crawford was frankly surprised that so many people were disturbed about an incident that had taken place so far away, and in New England at that. New Englanders had never seemed much interested in what happened to Carolina people.

But the Squire's voice grew hoarse trying to read all four pages of the newspaper to the people of the Waxhaws who could not read themselves. He had to recruit other public readers from among the few who were able to read. Young William Richardson Davie was one of the most popular readers, although he was often away at boarding school.

The Reverend Richardson, always feeling guilty that he was not doing enough for his parishioners, had now begun a school at the Waxhaw meetinghouse. Although most of the Waxhaw fathers felt their sons would be better off if they learned only reading, writing, and ciphering, the Reverend Richardson wanted to have an "academy" where the older students could also learn Greek and Latin. His godson Davie was already very accomplished in the "classical languages," because Richardson was determined to send the boy to college. The few colleges that existed in the provinces, and all the colleges back in the mother country, taught courses in Latin and Greek rather than in English.

Rob Jackson probably attended the Reverend Richardson's academy for a short while, although sitting stiffly in a classroom was pure torture for him. Andrew, as his mother had planned, began learning to read before he was five years old.

Frecklefaced Andy was no sissy. His brothers had seen to it that he was often roughed up and tumbled about. As he grew taller, Hugh and Rob discovered their scrappy little brother was not one to tangle with. At times his temper went far beyond brotherly fighting. The one thing Andrew could not tolerate was to be made fun of. When a boy laughed at him, he began to drool. If Andy tried to shout ugly names or holler down his opponent, his mouth filled with saliva and the drool ran down his chin. Then he became as furious as an enraged bull.

The nearest academy to the Jacksons and Crawfords was in the brand-new town of Charlotte, North Carolina province, about thirty miles to the north, where the village of Spratts used to be. When Mecklenburg County was formed in 1766, a group of men decided to start a new town and build a showy courthouse in it, so that their town would become the county seat. Having the court held in a town was sure to turn it into a city and bring money to all.

The men could find only enough bricks to build the first floor of the courthouse. The second floor was of logs, with log pillars ten feet high. A long building, it sat square in the center where Trade and Tryon streets crossed. The lower part was used as the market, bringing traffic of all kinds straight into the middle of town. An outside stairway led to the courthouse and meeting rooms upstairs.

Four times a year, on public days when lawyers and judges came to hold court, local people traveled to the county seat just to see a big crowd of people. Many played games of quoits or held target contests on the great expanse of courthouse lawn.

One of the first laws in Charlotte showed that this was to be a city that valued culture, even though it was not far from the frontier and its citizens were a little rough around the edges. The lawmakers voted against playing the game of "long bullets" in the street. This was disappointing to the young men of the town because the main street was an ideal spot for the game. Long bullets was played by two opposing teams, each trying to roll a large iron ball past the other's goal line. The game made walking in the street very risky for all but the most spry citizen.

Charlotte now had several wooden houses and shops. At his tailoring shop, John McNitt Alexander charged only seven shillings to make a man's greatcoat of broadcloth, although the customer also had to pay extra for the material, the thread for the buttonholes, and the buttons.

Most shops in Charlotte were costly but popular, especially with the ladies who had to make all of their own clothing.

Every time Uncle James or Squire Crawford traveled north from the Waxhaws up the post road, their wives and friends gave them long lists of items to buy at Jeremiah McCafferty's store. The store had all sorts of fabric, from persian, osnaburgs, and forest cloth to the more expensive calico that cost eight shillings for one yard. Although the prices were high for pins, buttons, thread, salt, and sugar, McCafferty knew that the Waxhaw ladies could not find what they needed at the country stores of Paw Creek, Sugar Creek, Rocky River, or Hopewell.

Charlotte's academy, called Queen's College, began in March 1771 with three tutors. The Reverend Richardson sent his godson William Richardson Davie there to learn Latin, Greek, philosophy, theology, and Hebrew, so he could do well in college. But an academy could not succeed without having a charter from His Majesty the King. Even though the academy was named for his wife, in a town named for his wife, the King refused to grant the charter. The president of the academy, Edmund Fanning, was not surprised. He said it was because the Church of England was afraid that having a Presbyterian school might woo the children of the town away from the state church.

The King may have had other reasons for refusing a charter for a school in the Carolinas. He was very angry because the people who lived in that part of North Carolina were protesting that no one in the Assembly represented the ordinary people—only the rich landowners. Early in May, Governor William Tryon, with his militiamen, had crushed a treasonous rebellion at Alamance Creek near Hillsborough. Then, too, the King was angry because the Stamp Act was not bringing in money. Even though some of the items taxed were very important to the stubborn colonists, they were still refusing to buy anything with a tax on it. What surprised the British rulers more, those colonists seemed to agree and stick together on avoiding taxed items, even though they lived a thousand miles from each other!

On December 13, 1770, a large group of rebel colonists had

gathered at what they called the "Liberty Tree" in Charles Town. They had been refusing to drink tea ever since the tax had been placed on it. Now they agreed not even to allow it to come into the port of Charles Town. Governor Bull was desperately trying to avoid trouble. As fast as he could, he had the tea cargo unloaded and put into storage. News about the "Liberty Tree" traveled to England on the next ship. It was one more burr under the British saddle. But it did not leak into the South Carolina *Gazette* until more than five months later, when Squire Crawford read about it to his delighted audience. They had all heard the story months before from eyewitnesses who lived in the Low Country, but knowing it was written in the *Gazette* made them feel their newspaper editor could be trusted to tell them the rebel news, even if it was somewhat late.

The Reverend Richardson's academy was a great success in the Waxhaws even without a charter. But the preacher never seemed satisfied with what he had accomplished in life. His godson Davie brought him much joy, but Nancy Richardson told Betty Jackson that her husband was often unhappy and depressed. She was not sure whether it was because the Church of England would not allow preachers of other faiths to marry young couples in their own churches, or because lately there had been so much fuss over church singing. Some of Richardson's flock wanted to sing the more tuneful Watts hymns, but others insisted that God intended only the Psalms to be sung. In addition, church people were starting to argue about such sins as gambling, young people who danced and played cards, drunkards, horseracing, and the people who did not go to church on Sundays.

Reverend Richardson took so many long, solitary rides that Nancy never knew when he would be home. During his travels, he started many small churches along the frontier. Sometimes he rode to the Catawba Indian village nearby. The friendly Catawbas politely listened to his preaching and told him stories about their enemies, the Cherokees. Then he rode off into the country west of the Catawba River and tried to convince the tall, fierce Cherokees that they should become Christians. Always he came back to Nancy more depressed than ever. He shut himself in his study for long hours at a time. Nancy knew better than to disturb him at his prayers, which seemed to be getting longer and longer.

William Davie had just gone off to Nassau Hall, a college in Prince Town, province of West Jersey, when tragedy came to the Richardson house. On a hot July day, Nancy had been to a quilting. She arrived home just as an old friend rode up on his horse.

"William Boyd, how good to see you," she greeted him. Boyd had ridden over from Rocky Creek to ask Richardson if he would preach to some people there. Nancy sent him up to knock on the study door. Boyd knocked softly, then more loudly. But there was no response. Not wanting to disturb the preacher at his prayers, Boyd peeped through the keyhole. The preacher was indeed on his knees, so Boyd tiptoed down the stairs. He visited with Nancy for awhile, but the preacher still did not come down. Finally, Nancy felt a little anxious, so she went up to his study.

A loud scream brought Boyd running up after her. Richardson was dead, on his knees, a leather strap around his throat. Had he been murdered? Or had he killed himself? Boyd told Nancy to call in some neighbors and have all the facts made known to them. These witnesses decided it was in the best interest of their church if they simply told people the preacher had died while saying his prayers.

Everyone in the Waxhaws was shocked. The preacher was only forty-two, and a robust, healthy-looking man. The story of how he died saying his prayers was added to and improved at every dinner table.

"He has always been subject to vapory disorders," said one of the preacher's friends, Archibald Simpson. "Lately his intellect seemed to fail."

The preacher was buried in the Waxhaw churchyard. He

left his plantation and ten negro slaves to Nancy, although he set aside enough money for William Davie to finish his college education at Prince Town.

He also left a small fortune, 346 pounds sterling, to buy religious books for the poor. Inside each book, he asked that these lines be written:

> *It is desired that no person will offer to sell this book, but as it is freely given, first read it with serious attention . . . and then lend or give it to their friend or neighbor. . . .*

5

Scrappy Redhead

ANDY JACKSON rode his horse to school. It was a grass pony, bred in the Waxhaws, but no longer of great value. For their own uses, grown-ups now wanted thoroughbred horses raised in Virginia, or on the gentlemen's plantations in the Low Country, and were willing to pay high prices for them.

At first the older boys told Andy to follow a respectful distance behind them. But a few days of riding in their dust soon had him spoiling for a fight. He began finding other paths to school. Sometimes he made a trail through the woods. Other days he rode through the swamps. It pleased him to be able to fade into the background and disappear silently like an Indian. He was a good horseman. Some said he rode as if his horse were an extension of his own body.

School began on schedule in the Waxhaw meetinghouse, where church met on Sundays. William Humphries came to take the place of the preacher-schoolmaster Richardson.

At school the pupils had to use a rough board table as a desk. They had no blackboards or chalk, and only the teacher had books. Their paper was rough and dark. Mr. Humphries gave each pupil some pieces cut the same size and showed him how to stitch a seam down the center to make his own "book." Then he taught them how to cut a pen from a large quill and to make their own ink.

School was a noisy place, with pupils of all ages reciting their different lessons aloud. At any moment the master might bend down from behind a student and listen to that boy's recitation. A mistake was corrected immediately with a hard thump on the head.

Just as Betty Jackson had thought, Andy showed genius at reading and working with numbers. Unfortunately, spelling was not important to either Andy or his teacher. No one had a dictionary, and Webster had not yet written his. Each person spelled words exactly the way they sounded to his ear. Even Uncle James Crawford spelled his name "Crafford," and if Uncle George McKemey had been able to read, he would have seen his own name spelled McAmey, McCamy, and other ways. In all his life, Andrew Jackson never did learn to spell.

He had learned at the age of five not to cry when tormented. His mother told Mrs. Polk that she once found Andy crying.

"Stop that!" she had commanded. "Don't let me see you cry again. Girls are made for crying, not boys."

"Then what are boys made for?" Andy asked through tears.

"They're made to fight."

Betty Jackson may have been sorry she answered in just that way, because her son took her at her word. In fact, he never quite learned to control his passions. When he was in a rage he choked up and could not speak. The older boys made fun of him. When they laughed at him, Andy's face twisted with fury. Then he attacked his tormentors.

He was tall and swift on his feet. He could win footraces and jumping matches with the other boys, but he was too lightweight for wrestling.

"I could throw him three times out of four," said George McWhorter, one of the boys at Mr. Humphries's school with Andy. "But he never stayed throwed. He was dead game."

Upcountry Carolina was no place for a well-bred gentleman or a macaroni in lace and velvet. In fact, wealthy Charles Town planters never ventured up the dirt roads that led to the Waxhaws. Most of the Jacksons' neighbors were Scotch-

Irish Presbyterians who had lived awhile in the back country
of Pennsylvania before moving south. They had never known
luxuries and were quite used to putting up with discomforts.

A few were starting to make a fortune, like Squire Crawford,
who had had the good sense to get out of trying to farm the
red clay soil and start raising beef cattle instead. When neighbors had arguments and fights, they had to be settled without
the help of the law. The nearest courthouse was miles away,
and unless that courthouse was in a county seat, court was
held only a few times a year. The local people singled out the
few respected men in their area who had some schooling and
a sense of fair play. They labeled these men "Squire," and
went to them to have their arguments settled.

Old folks had worked hard to improve their farms, but after
their sons inherited the land, the younger generation seemed
to be more interested in frolicking than work. Even the boys
in their teens were indulging in amusements their fathers never
knew of.

Mrs. Thomas Polk told Betty Jackson one day that she did
not know what young men were coming to. The Polks of
Charlotte had four sons. Charles, William, James, and Ezekiel
were turning her hair white, she confided.

Mr. Polk owned a mill and kept a store in the village. Once
he mentioned that he had never been robbed, although there
was so much talk of highway robberies. His son Charles overheard the remark and a wicked grin lit up his face. The next
week, Mr. Polk was traveling along the highway alone with
a large amount of money, when a suspicious-looking man
spurred his horse straight at him.

Polk grabbed for his pistols, but the masked stranger was
too quick for him. One look at the bulge pointed straight at
him from under the stranger's jacket, and Mr. Polk handed
over his heavy purse. When he reached home, his sons asked
him why he was so upset.

"This day I was robbed," said their father.

"What? A fine figure of a man like you?" Charles asked.
"There must have been several men."

"No, just one."

Charles handed his father the money and confessed that it was he who had robbed him. Polk stared at his son and demanded, "Did you not endanger your father's life by presenting a gun at my breast?"

"No, sir," Charles answered smiling, totally thoughtless that his father might have had a heart attack out on the road. "It was only my mother's brass candlestick that I took from the mantelpiece."

Mrs. Polk had no sooner finished telling this story to Betty Jackson than she began to complain about another son. Ezekiel Polk and a friend were out in a wagon one day when they saw a gentleman in a sulky. Gentlemen were not often seen in the neighborhood, and a swift little sulky pulled by a beautiful horse was even more rare. The young men offered the gentleman a drink and talked a few minutes. Learning that he was not from Charlotte, and therefore not likely to be a threat to them, they decided to have their fun with him.

"We have this way," Ezekiel began, "that we like strangers to dance for us."

The two boys cracked their riding whips for music while the stranger "danced." Finally they stopped. The stranger said in a friendly way that after such a jig, he would like to offer them a drink. While opening his sulky box, he drew out a pair of pistols and pointed them at his tormenters.

"It's not a good idea to play tricks on strangers," he said coldly. "Now you shall dance for me."

The boys danced until they almost dropped.

"I never had such a sweat in my life," said Ezekiel.

Every big boy Andy knew could handle a musket or a pistol. They had gone hunting with their fathers and learned how to load guns. Hugh and Rob had taught Andy how to use their musket as soon as he could lift it off the ground. One day some of Andy's friends loaded a musket for him to shoot. Andy had not seen the loading of it, or he would have known they had packed it too full, clear to the muzzle.

"See if you can hit that stump," said a large boy. Andy did not notice the others behind him, hiding their grins. Or if he did notice, he thought they were snickering because he was too weak to lift the musket and fire from a standing position. He'd show them. He took aim and fired. The recoil was so powerful it sent him sprawling on the ground.

The pain in his shoulder was nothing to the pain he felt when the first boy looked about to laugh. Andy Jackson sprang to his feet, a shock of red hair partially hiding the blue eyes that flashed with anger.

"By God," he shouted. "If one of you laughs, I'll kill him."

Mrs. Jackson saw to it that her boys, especially Andy, sat by her every Sunday for the two-hour church service. She might have had more luck turning her Andy into a preacher if only the Reverend Richardson had lived longer. But the circuit preachers who rode over from Fishing Creek and Bullocks Creek to give sermons were never able to inspire her son.

All he remembered about those painfully long Sundays in church was the sight of his mother's Bible, covered with a checked cloth to preserve it, lying in her lap. Years later, when he was an old man, Andrew finally joined the church and covered his own Bible in cloth with a checked pattern.

After church service the people gathered around Squire Crawford to see whether he had a newspaper that week. But not every church member listened to the printed news. Some of the news going about the church on wagging tongues was more curious.

The story leaked out about how the Reverend Richardson had died. He could not have killed himself, many people insisted. It had to be murder! Nancy Richardson had remarried. To George Dunlap. And without even waiting for a decent length of time after her husband was set in the grave. They needed no trial or judge in the Waxhaws. The church people themselves would see that justice was done.

"A dead body condemns its own murderer."

The speaker was Archibald Davie, father of William Richardson Davie, Nancy's godson.

Betty Jackson hurried to support her friend, but ugly stories circulated swiftly in the Waxhaws, even though the tellers of them lived far apart. A year after he died, a group from the church demanded that the body of the Reverend Richardson be dug up and a "test" made.

One of the superstitions brought over from Scotland and Ireland was that if a murderer touched a dead body, it would bleed. One day most of the congregation stood at the Waxhaw churchyard while the body was brought out of the grave. The coffin was opened. Nancy, terrified, was told to touch the forehead of her dead husband. But she could not bear to open her eyes. She reached out blindly and gently touched cold skin.

Suddenly, Archibald Davie seized her hand and jabbed her finger down hard on the skull. She shrieked in dread, her eyes still closed.

But the witnesses saw what they had come to see. There was no blood.

6

Tory Tea and Hot Letters

On May 10, 1773, the British Parliament passed the Tea Act. But it was almost winter before the Waxhaws people learned about it. As usual, the news came up from the Low Country by way of the cattledrivers who had been celebrating in Charles Town.

As soon as he was able to get a newspaper and read about the Tea Act, Squire Crawford explained to his regular audience that the British East India Tea Company had gone deeply in debt—all because people had refused to buy tea. This Tea Act was supposed to help the company, but what it really did was hurt every small shopkeeper there in the provinces. The tea company could now sell tea very cheaply. But everyone else had to pay a tax, so they had to try to sell it at a higher price.

The Waxhaw people looked around at their neighbors. Plenty of them were Tories, but which ones? From this day onward, all those who still drank tea would be at the top of the suspected list.

In school Andy Jackson and the other pupils had not learned much geography. Now their teacher decided they should see a map of the colonies and learn to read it. Maps were rare and very expensive, but he found one in Reverend Richardson's library.

Mr. Humphries taught his pupils what little he knew about the larger cities in the new world. Boston, New York, and the largest city, Philadelphia, were all miles away from the Waxhaws, but they were all part of the same country. He pointed out the roads and seaports that bound the country together.

Andy and the others learned that Boston and New York had street lights that brightened the city at night so much that men and women could go out walking. In Charlotte, thirty miles away, night-time parties were usually held only on moonlit nights so people could find their way home. The State House in Philadelphia was the largest building in the country, and it had a clock on its side so everyone in town always knew what time it was. In the Waxhaws, when a farmer's clock stopped ticking, he had to find out from an almanac what time the sun rose on the next day, then stand outside until the sun came up and run indoors to set his clock.

Meanwhile, Andy was learning a great deal about the geography of the Waxhaw area. He and Rob rode their horses along every Catawba Indian trail. But they had been warned to keep their distance from the Indians and their village of Tuckahoe.

Andy had never known his Uncle Hugh back in Ireland, or heard his tales of the Catawba Indians who had scouted bravely for the British fifteen years before. The Catawbas Andy met in the Waxhaws were no longer the proud and gentle hunters Hugh had known. Years of diseases brought by the white man had killed many of them off. All other Indian tribes had turned against the Catawbas for siding with the white men. The Cherokees killed their cattle, not quite daring to attack the tribe that had the white man's protection, but hating them because of it. The plantation owners especially valued the Catawbas because the Indians had an uncanny ability to track down their runaway slaves.

Andy had often wanted to ride into the Indian village. He would like to have explored the strange-shaped straw hut that stood like a giant loaf of bread in the center. But their cousin James Crawford had warned the Jackson boys away.

"The Catawbas told their sworn enemies the Cherokees that they would turn their men into women if they captured them. How'd you like to be changed into a girl?"

Andy could not imagine anything worse than being a girl and having to wear dresses like Sarah, Mary, and Isabella Crawford. Not even the older girls were allowed to ride free across the land as he and Rob were riding now. Besides, his grown-up cousin James was Andy's hero. He would do anything James told him to do. They turned their horses away.

Toward the end of 1773, the King's postman may have noticed that his mailbag was heavier. More people were writing letters to their relations in other parts of the country. A letter traveled to Philadelphia from Boston and returned in six weeks. Then Benjamin Franklin was put in charge of the northern postal region. After that, a letter's round trip took only three weeks. But no Ben Franklin headed the southern postal region. Letters sent to Charles Town from Philadelphia took forty-three days to travel four hundred miles. Letters that traveled by ship might reach Charles Town in less than two weeks, but if the wind blew the wrong way, a ship might carry a letter even more slowly than the King's Post.

That was not fast enough for important mail. The British were coming down hard on those rebels who lived around Boston. The rebels and the patriots were now the same people. To the Tories and the British, they were rebels. To the Jacksons and Crawfords, they were the patriots. When the New Englanders decided to take a stand about the Tea Act, they wanted other patriots to know how they felt. But the King's Post was not the way to spread the word.

Instead of mailing letters, they formed "Committees of Correspondence" to write letters to patriots in other cities all along the coast. They sent those letters by special courier— as quickly as possible from one city to the next. The best riders were chosen to ride for this early "pony express." One was Paul Revere. In only eleven days, he made the round trip between Boston and Philadelphia. From that city, other riders went out with secret messages.

The riders carrying the letters to Charles Town and beyond had to go along the worst roads of all. In addition to being rutted and uncared for, the southern roads had a habit of running out suddenly in dead ends. Then the riders spent valuable time retracing their routes to try different paths. Along the way they had to keep their missions secret. Tories were everywhere, ready to report anything suspicious to the British militia.

"The colonists are rustics," said the British governors. "Most of them cannot read or write. They can't organize any sort of resistance."

But the British were wrong. The committees managed to pass the word all along the American seacoast: Watch for a British ship that would soon appear at the nearest seaport to unload the expensive British tea. By the time the ships arrived, the colonists were ready for them.

In Boston, a group of patriots dressed up as Indians boarded a ship and tossed the tea into the harbor. In Edenton, North Carolina, a group of women met the ship and threw the tea overboard. In New York, the Sons of Liberty dumped tea in the river. Patriots in Annapolis burned the tea and also the ship that brought it. British soldiers managed to unload the tea in Greenwich, West Jersey, but the patriots burned down the storehouse.

In Charles Town, the Tories had seen unusual activity around the Liberty Tree. They warned Governor William Bull of South Carolina that the rebels were plotting some mischief. When the ship appeared offshore, he ordered its captain to wait before landing. Then, on a dark night when the tide was high, and there was no danger of running aground on Charles Town's tricky sandbars, the ship entered port. It was unloaded and the tea placed under guard in a storehouse before the patriots could organize. There it stayed two and a half years.

Then the patriots liberated the tea, auctioned it off, and used the money to fight the British.

When news of the tea parties reached England, the King was furious. He demanded that the rebels be punished. Parliament passed several laws to show the colonists in America what would happen when they refused to obey the King.

The colonists called this latest set of laws "The Intolerable Acts." The letter committees got busy again, writing to friends in all the thirteen colonies and telling them what these latest laws would mean in Massachusetts and how the liberty of all the colonists was threatened. Squire Crawford kept the Waxhaws people informed.

The port of Boston was to be closed up. After June first, all ships were ordered to land at Salem, Massachusetts, to unload. The people of Massachusetts were no longer allowed to hold their town meetings. And the colonists were told they must take British soldiers into their homes and give them bedding, firewood, drink, soap, and candles. The new laws made it seem as if the entire province had been put in prison.

"Imagine what would happen to us if the King should close our port of Charles Town," Andy's teacher told his students. "Or if you had to take British soldiers into your homes to live."

It was not hard to imagine. Most people in the Waxhaws grew enough food to feed themselves, and they needed no luxuries. But the people of Boston were going to have less food, and they might not have enough woolen cloth to keep warm in the winter.

Andy Jackson was not even sure where he and his mother would live. Rob now worked at Squire Robert Crawford's with Hugh. Aunt Jennet had died, and in 1774 Uncle James Crawford had gone to live with one of his sons. The house now belonged to James, Jr., Andy's favorite cousin. James and his wife Christiana had small children of their own. James was so close to Andrew all his life that it seems reasonable to say that he must have provided the Jacksons with a small building of their own to call home. Betty Jackson was an expert weaver, since her family in Ireland had been in the wool business. Many people in the Waxhaws had bought Mrs. Jackson's linen and wool cloth, and she was happy to have the money it brought in.

Long before June, when the port of Boston was to be closed, the post road was filled with wagons heading for New England. From the Low Country plantations came loads of rice; from the Waxhaws, corn and barley. Squire Crawford's cattledrivers headed northward with fresh meat on the hoof.

All over the colonies, June 1, 1774, was marked by mourning. Every church bell in the new world was muffled and gave out the sorrowful sounds of death.

In Philadelphia, one boy of thirteen wrote in his diary:

This being the Day appointed for Blocking up the Harbor of Boston, the Bells were Muffled and most of the Cityzens shut up their stores, Quakers excepted. The Prespeterans keep this Day as a fast. Almost every Sea Vessel in this Harbour had her flags half mast high.

The mourning did not stop after the harbor was blocked. Southern patriots felt guilty about enjoying their horseracing, gambling, cockfighting, or even going to the theater. They stopped all the sports they had enjoyed in their leisure time. In October, one of the best companies of actors in Charles Town sailed for the West Indies because the theaters at home were empty.

The rebel patriots of the town were busy planning a New Year's surprise for their governor.

7

A Potful of Patriots

GOVERNOR WILLIAM BULL perspired underneath his powdered wig, even though it was cold on January 16, 1775.

Before him sat the men of the South Carolina Assembly. Many of them had smiling faces, only partly hidden behind their hands. They knew, he realized suddenly. Another trickle of sweat ran out from under the wig.

"I have the misfortune to report," he began stiffly, "the very extraordinary and alarming disappearance of about eight hundred guns, two hundred cutlasses, and sixteen hundred pounds of powder . . . and minor stores from the arsenal."

Governor Bull was not hated. Many of the rebels had seen that he was more sympathetic to them than he ought to be. But his salary was paid by the Crown, and there was no doubt that he would be on the side of the British.

"There is every reason to suppose," one member of the Commons spoke very seriously, "that some inhabitants of this colony may have taken this step because of the alarming accounts of the doings of the government of Great Britain."

More hands went up to hide grins. Every man in the room knew exactly what had happened to the military stores. As soon as the governor could leave the Assembly with some sort of dignity, he resigned his office. Immediately the British government replaced the good man with Lord William Campbell.

Campbell was a deadly threat to the patriots and a former British Navy man. No one had any doubts about whose side he was on. The Tories and Loyalists were delighted. And the patriots were relieved. Campbell was going to be a much easier man to hate.

Betty Jackson still hoped there would not be war. Through the cold winter, she spun flax to sell and visited with her friend Nancy. The boring duties saved for women made Mrs. Jackson miserable. If there was to be war, she would like to be in the fighting.

While the women tried not to think of the future, the men of the Waxhaws prepared for war. Squire Crawford had a gang out repairing the roads and clearing trails for new roads. Over small creeks, they built bridges sturdy enough to stand a wagon's weight. A constant stream of wagons now traveled northward with food and other supplies.

War came suddenly, like death. Express riders carried the news of the Lexington and Concord fight, and word that the new governor, Lord William Campbell, had moved his office from the capitol to a ship in Charles Town harbor.

As soon as Campbell had moved, the patriots began preparing to defend the city. Every mechanic and laborer, and great numbers of slaves brought down from the country, went to work. They took the lead from church and house windows to melt down for musket balls. They mounted one hundred cannons around different parts of the harbor. A large group had begun to build a fort on Sullivan's Island, just north of the harbor entrance, and worked day and night to finish it.

The upcountry men knew what to do. They organized a militia company of their own. Squire Robert Crawford, now forty-eight, was elected captain. Far to the north, another group of men were already deciding on George Washington as the chief of the Continental Forces.

Robert Crawford was lucky to enlist his own regiment so

easily. To be a captain, a man had to collect his own men in any way he could.

One day, for example, a well-mannered man, Bernard Elliott, arrived in the Waxhaws with four helpers. He had a drummer, a fifer, a fiddle player, and a well-dressed sergeant. When this strange team stopped at a tavern on the post road near where Andy Jackson lived, they played Irish and military music. Elliott was impressed with the rawboned country men who stopped to see what was going on. The new captain offered to buy a drink for any man who would sign up to be in his regiment. The Upcountry men were impressed. Elliott even carried hard money, the kind that clanked in one's pocket, to pay the men who enlisted.

"Won't you join?" Elliott asked one athletic-looking man.

The man looked at the captain and down at his silk stockings, and muttered, "I never could serve under a man that I could lick."

Elliott suggested a short, rough fight. After a few hard punches and a knockdown, the man enlisted. So did many others who had come to watch the fun.

In the nearby town of Charlotte, men joined together one night in May 1775 to sign their names to a list of resolutions. They called it simply the Mecklenburg County Resolutions. They sent it by courier to Philadelphia, and many of those ideas found their way into a more important declaration a year later.

The war stayed in the north all summer. The Squire kept his Waxhaw neighbors up on the news as often as he could find news. But now, muster days, when his newly formed militia drilled, were more important than reading the news. Younger readers, including Andy, had to take on the job of reading about the capture of Fort Ticonderoga and the battle at Breed's Hill.

Real war came to the south that summer.

The British expected an easy landing in Charles Town because so many Tories were in the south. Tories had told them that the fort at Sullivan's Island was only half finished in May and had only twenty-five guns.

On June 1, 1776, fifty sails appeared off the harbor of Charles Town. No question about whose sails they were. The Continental Navy at that time had only one ship and a captured brig.

Captain Crawford's militia marched to Charles Town. Near the city, the men found the road jammed with carriages, wagons, and horses. Wives and children were fleeing for their lives. They looked as if they had been dumped quickly into any vehicle with wheels. Their arms were clasped around odd-shaped bundles of valuables to be hidden in the country.

As the militia neared the town gates, Crawford and his officers on horseback had to push the crowd aside to get their men into the city. They marched to their assigned position in Lynch's meadow in the Neck. Crawford had supplied his men with the new long rifles. Rifles were much more accurate than muskets, although they took much longer to load and reload.

All the action, however, took place at the fort on Sullivan's Island, six miles away. The fort was in charge of Colonel William Moultrie, an old Indian fighter. Moultrie's men needed every minute they had to prepare their unfinished fort for what was ahead. General Charles Lee, in charge of defending Charles Town, had just said the fort looked like a "slaughter pen" to him.

Luckily the wind was blowing from the wrong direction. The square-rigged British ships could not enter until the wind changed. Two of them tried on June 9, but both ran aground. A food supply ship was a total loss, but the other escaped when the tide rose. Another ship anchored off Sullivan's Island, so close to the fort that its officers could watch Moultrie's men working day and night to build up their fort.

On June 28 the wind changed. Eight ships of war sailed close to Moultrie's half-finished fort on the island. They anchored and swung around broadside to train their guns directly on the fort. Most of the heavy shells fell in the center of the fort. The center was still deep sand and a good-sized swamp, because the men had spent all their time on the seaside walls. The shells landed without doing harm, while the fort's cannons did a great deal of damage to the ships.

"In the hottest of the action," one of the British sailors said later, "a cannon ball passed so near Sir Peter Parker's coat tail as to tear it off, together with his clothes, clear to the buff."

Captain Bernard Elliott was on the island with the regiment he had recruited from the Upcountry. One of his sergeants, named McDaniel, lost his shoulder and stomach to a British cannonball. But when he fell, Captain Elliott said later, the sergeant shouted, "Fight on, my brave boys! Don't let liberty expire with me today!"

Finally the British gave up. Their ships left on the outgoing tide. They had lost more than a hundred men. A dozen Americans were killed; two dozen were wounded.

The Waxhaw militia marched home with hundreds of war stories to tell. But when asked if any of them were wounded, they had to say their worst injuries were from the mosquitoes in Lynch's meadow.

With renewed hope, Captain Crawford kept his militia busy sending provisions north to General Washington's Continental army. Between trips, he held muster days to keep his men fit. Hugh Jackson often rode as a messenger between militia companies.

Rob Jackson now rode with the cattledrovers. Crawford's beef cattle were very important to the army up north. Sometimes Rob took them to the Cowpens to be fattened, but just as often nearby farmers had ground that was exhausted from raising the same crop and needed fertilizing. The best way to make their land fertile again was to "cowpen" it. They fenced it in and filled it with cattle to fertilize it naturally, and in a year or two the soil was as good as new.

The war did not return to the south for two and a half years. But when it did, the world that young Andrew Jackson had known and loved came to a sudden end.

Newspapers were hard to get now. The rags from which the paper was made were needed elsewhere. The British had stopped delivering the mail at the end of 1775. When a special courier arrived one August afternoon at the Squire's, word passed quickly through the Waxhaw settlement.

Andrew Jackson remembered that day all his life. He was almost nine and a half years old and was considered one of the "good readers." He could manage even long words without having to spell them out. The Squire, now Captain Crawford, solemnly handed him the Pennsylvania *Gazette* dated July 10, 1776. About forty people had collected to see what the courier had brought.

"This day you shall be my public reader, Andrew," said the Squire. "Only a young person will be able to get all the way through this document without getting hoarse."

Andrew stood up on the top step and began reading in his shrill voice:

In C O N G R E S S, July 4, 1776.
A   D E C L A R A T I O N
By the R E P R E S E N T A T I V E S of the
U N I T E D   S T A T E S of A M E R I C A, in
G E N E R A L   C O N G R E S S assembled.

H E N, in the Course of human Events, it becomes necessary for one People to dissolve the political Bands which have connected them with another, and to assume among the Powers of the Earth, the separate and equal Station to which the Laws of Nature and of Nature's God entitle them, a decent Respect to the Opinions of Mankind requires that they should declare the causes which impel them to the Separation.

We hold these Truths to be self-evident, that all Men are created equal . . .

8

Cockfights and Duels

"Haw. . . . Haw. . . . Whoa there. . . . Haw!"

The drovers' commands coming from Andrew's slim frame sounded piercing. But the cattle started moving down the road, bound for Charleston.

Betty Jackson watched with mixed feelings. She was not happy to see her brightest boy join a motley gang of dusty drovers. He was eleven that summer and had waited years for this day when it would be his turn to join the men.

He was an excellent rider. His mother had never worried about him on a horse. But she was worried about his schooling. The small school at Waxhaw meeting often disbanded because there was no one to teach the pupils. Mrs. Jackson had no extra money to send Andrew away to school, where she would have to pay for him to live with strangers. She longed to send her youngest to a good school, so he could go to a famous university like the one in West Jersey where Nancy's godson, William Richardson Davie, had gone.

Andy insisted that he could pay his own way. After all, Rob had earned good hard money going on a cattle drive.

At last his mother agreed. The war for independence was still raging furiously up north. Who could tell what the next few months would bring if the British tried to enter Charleston

harbor again? Better for Andy to go now and gain the experience. From far down the road Betty could see the dust kicked up by the moving cattle, and imagined she still heard Andy's shrill "Whoa. . . . Haw. . . ." She smiled once, remembering that Andy had told her the Indian word for "cows" was "Wo-haw," the only English sounds the Indians had heard when a cattle drive passed them.

After the drivers reached the city and delivered the cattle to the buyer, Andrew had plenty of time to look around. The men who were so friendly to him on the way down all took off in different directions with mumbled excuses. He saw some go into the nearest tavern, but he was surprised that so many seemed to have lady friends to visit in the city.

Charles Town was larger than he had imagined in his wildest dreams. Houses larger than Captain Crawford's—on every street. City parks planted with bright flowers. Ladies in everyday dresses more beautiful than any his mother had ever owned. And gentlemen who wore clothing made of soft kinds of material.

The rich planters kept their families in the city during the hot summer. The air was healthier by the sea than at their plantations. Andy probably saw the cream of Charles Town society as he rode slowly down the tree-shaded streets.

His feeling of joy at watching life in the big city mingled with a new feeling he had never known. He must look like a simple "country pumpkin" to them, even though he rode one of the Squire's best horses. He had always fancied he cut quite a figure in the new woolen breeches and watch coat his mother had woven for him. Now he had the uncomfortable feeling that even the street urchins were laughing behind his back.

Local people now called their city "Charleston," although the name had not been officially changed yet. The new name sounded much less British, and people wanted to forget their town was named for a British king. Other names in the land had changed, too. Prince Town, where William Richardson

Davie had gone to college, was now called "Princeton." Even in Charlotte, the name of the academy had changed from Queen's College and Queen's Museum to "Liberty Hall."

Back at the cattledrovers' camp, Andy found that many of the men had already seen enough of their lady friends. They were crowded around a cockfighting pit, cheering their favorite fighting roosters. The two gamecocks had just finished chasing each other around the ring, to the anguished howls of the men who had bet money on the loser. Feathers now flew in every direction as they closed together.

"Blood!" hollered several of the men, as if the cocks could understand them.

Andrew watched while the two cocks tore at each other, kicking with the knives on their spurs. He thought the largest one must win, but he was wrong. The smaller cock was the fightingest and could get at the underparts of the big one. When one finally lay almost dead in the ring, a great cheer went up and the men collected their winning bets.

Next morning Andy rode home behind the other men. Most had very bad headaches and were not feeling as friendly as when they had ridden down. To himself Andy made a vow. The next time he came to this big city, he would not be wearing the clothes of a cattledrover.

Captain Crawford paid his men at the end of the cattle drive. He had known the men's families would not see any of the money if he had paid them before they went to the big city. Andrew proudly took home his earnings to his mother.

Betty Jackson had already decided how to spend Andy's earnings and had chosen the school. The Reverend Francis Cummins kept a "classical" boarding school on the other side of the Catawba River. No records of the school remain, nor is it even known how long Andy stayed there.

He must have improved his Latin, because he could not have studied law without it. But no polish from the classical school rubbed off on Andy's raw exterior. He saved no neatly written copybooks for future scholars to admire. Only one piece of paper still exists from that year at boarding school. Andrew must have given it some importance to have saved it all his life:

A MEMORANDUM HOW TO FEED A COCK BEFORE YOU HIM FIGHT. Take and give him some Pickle Beaf Cut fine 3 times a Day and give him sweet Milk Instead of water to Drink   give him Dry Indien corn that hase been Dryn Up in smoke   give him lighte wheat Bread Soked in sweet Milk   feed him as Much as he Can Eat for Eaight Days   Orrange Town in Orange County March the 22d 79
Mr. Mabee Merchant

Andrew was to leave the Cummins school with his spelling as terrible as ever and with a new way to fight.

Dueling was the gentleman's way to fight. Even the reason for fighting was gentlemanly. A man challenged another to a duel to protect his honor. No gentleman ever struck another with his fists at Cummins. That was strictly prohibited for any reason, even among grown-up gentlemen, Andrew learned to his surprise. Not even giving an apology before witnesses could be accepted for such an insult.

For Andrew Jackson, who was used to flailing out with his fists first, this seemed like a hard rule. Then he saw that dueling worked to his advantage, as he had seldom won a fistfight or wrestling match. When one boy hit another at the Cummins school, the insult was settled in one way only. The boy who had struck the blow handed over a cane to be used on his back by the injured party, and at the same time begged his pardon. This dreadful turn of events was one that Andy could not stomach.

The boys at Cummins often had duels for real or imagined insults. First the offended person challenged his opponent. Then each boy appointed one or two seconds. In a grown-up duel, the seconds loaded the pistols. But at school, the seconds just watched to see that the fight was fair.

The boy who was challenged was allowed to select the place,

time, the weapons to be used, and the distance apart for the duellists. The seconds tried only halfheartedly to talk the two angry boys out of fighting. After all, it was not a fight to the death, like a real duel. The seconds' duty was to examine the weapons chosen, usually sticks or stones, and to measure the distance between the fighters at the start.

The duel ended when one person was "wounded" or made an apology. In a real duel, any wound bad enough to "agitate the nerves and make the hand shake" always ended the business for the day.

9

Charleston Falls

ANDREW RODE slowly down the road toward Land's Ford. So intent was he on solving his own problems that he hardly noticed the fine spring day.

His largest worry was how to tell his mother that he wanted no more of conjugating Latin verbs or preparing to be a preacher. His young body rebelled in a most unholy way against the many fast days Francis Cummins had expected of his students. Preachers at boarding schools were always finding reasons to have a fast day instead of providing a good solid dinner. Andrew longed for a heaping plate of the stewed chicken served on Sundays at Crawford's.

He supposed he would also have to explain the new clothes on his back, since his mother knew he had no money. That might be harder to make clear. He did not want to come right out and tell her the boys at the classical school were children when it came to simple gambling. But the truth was none of them had even played rattle and roll until Andy had shown them how. He had won the clothes fair and square. Only one voice had dared to say that Andy cheated, and that boy now wore a small scar from a gentlemanly duel.

Andrew had found a cockfighting pit at a nearby farm where the wealthier boys dropped some money, betting on which gamecock would win. But they never bet on the fightingest rooster. Andrew had taught them many new words that he had learned from the cattledrovers. On the whole, Andy had done quite a lot this year to fill in the gaps of the Cummins Academy curriculum.

He crossed the ford, although a freshet had made the water rise almost to his horse's belly, and headed up the river road toward Captain Robert Crawford's.

Long before Andrew reached the entrance road, he could see great activity. Crawford was now a major, and he had started a public army station on his own plantation.

William Richardson Davie was there, too. He had graduated from Princeton and returned to the Waxhaws. The war had spoiled his plans to study religion at the university in Scotland.

"One less preacher in the world," Andy thought. This news might come in handy when he started explaining to his mother.

Davie had gone to study law in Salisbury, North Carolina. While he was there, he had raised a cavalry company to join with the Waxhaw militia. He was their lieutenant.

When Andrew finally found Hugh, he too was dressed as a soldier.

"I'm a private, now," Hugh said proudly. If Andy needed any proof that he had been living in another world while at the boarding school, this was it. The whole world had been preparing for war while he was reading about Julius Caesar!

The summer of 1779 was deadly hot, and the humid air was filled with diseases. The heavy British uniforms were not designed for fighting in such humid conditions, and soldiers were dropping from heat exhaustion. They were under orders to stop the supply of food that was going to General Washington's Continental Army from the southern planters. In order to do that, they had to take the south, but with an overland army. The British did not want to try sailing into the harbor of Charleston again. They expected their job to be easy, because there were so many Loyalists in the south.

But being a Loyalist was no longer a healthy way to live. Loyalists were families who had been loyal to their King, just as they had been taught all their lives. From their cradles they had learned that the King could do no wrong. Now he was sending soldiers to kill his own people. Many asked themselves if they really were on the right side after all.

At the same time, their rebellious patriot neighbors made life miserable for the Loyalists, calling them the ugly name of "Tory" and trying to make them change their loyalty. "Hunting for Tories" was a popular sport along the Catawba frontier. When one was caught, the patriots usually gave him a chance to change his loyalties and give an oath of allegiance to their cause. The prize, if he took the oath, was not having his home burned down. But just as often, a captured Tory was tied over the limb of a bent-down sapling until he remembered the names of other Tories for the "hunters" to go after.

Some Tories had already decided, now that real war had come, that they would do better to join those who wanted an independent country. The British did not find as many Loyalists in the south as they had hoped to find.

By summer, the British had moved up the coast from Florida and now controlled Savannah and Augusta, Georgia. They began marching up the post road toward Charleston.

Major Crawford's militia started south to join up with General Benjamin Lincoln. Captain Davie's new company of horse joined them. Hugh Jackson, Andy's big brother, marched with their cousins, William and Joseph Crawford. The Crawfords' older brother, James, sent along a wagon filled with supplies and a hired driver.

The British almost entered Charleston, then for some reason turned back south again. Only the rear of the British army felt the sting of the Waxhaw militia, at a place called Stono Ferry, not far from Charleston, on June 20, 1779.

By that time, even the southerners were suffering terribly from the parching heat. On the march, Hugh Jackson was very sick from sunstroke and had a high fever. Major Crawford ordered him to remain in camp during the attack. But after the others had left, Hugh followed behind on the double.

At first the battle went well. Eliza Wilkinson, a young girl who lived nearby, said, "While we were at breakfast, we heard cannon towards Stono Ferry roaring in a horrid manner. We immediately quit the table and ran out of doors." But the British had protected themselves well, and the cannons had no effect.

Lieutenant William Richardson Davie made a bold cavalry charge, reckless and heroic, and a boost to every Waxhaw man's morale. Then Davie was wounded in the thigh. Drummers began beating a retreat, but the injured Davie had fallen from his horse. A private from another company saw him struggling to remount and falling back to the ground. He ran over and boosted Davie up on his horse. The Waxhaw militia retreated in good order, taking their wounded with them.

After the battle, Davie spent some time in the hospital at Charleston, but he recovered. One hundred and thirty British soldiers at the ferry did not recover. Three hundred Americans died. One died of "excessive heat and fatigue" after the battle. He was Hugh Jackson.

Hugh's monument stands in the cemetery at the Waxhaw church, but he was probably buried with the others who died that day. The Waxhaw men had to travel fast to care for their wounded and could not be burdened by returning the dead. Many of the Waxhaw men were so disheartened that they quit and returned home after the battle. The sickly season had arrived, and both armies in the south found cool spots for refuge through July and August.

Andrew and Robert were impatient now to grow up and join Crawford's regiment. They hung around the encampment at his plantation, grateful for every small errand they could run. Robert rode as messenger between camps.

The winter passed quietly enough in the south. But Major Crawford kept his men in good shape. William Richardson Davie, now a captain, returned from the hospital with good news. He had authority from the state of North Carolina to raise a troop of cavalry and two companies of mounted infantry. The bad news was that they gave him no money. Davie had to sell his own estate to raise money for his troops' equipment.

Early in January 1780, Major Crawford heard that General Clinton had left New York with a large army. No doubt where he was heading! Crawford warned his men. If the weather was favorable, ships carrying a large British army might land near Charleston within ten days.

But the weather was not good. Storms drove the ships off course, and they lost sight of each other. All the cavalry horses drowned. Several ships were lost, including one that carried the heaviest cannons.

Rob and Andrew begged to go along with the militia to Charleston. But the major, still upset over losing Hugh, forbade it. The new preacher, Mr. Craighead, with the help of Betty Jackson, managed to get Andrew back into school after the excitement of helping the militia take off.

Crawford and his men had plenty of time to reach Charleston. They joined General Benjamin Lincoln's men already holed up in the city.

January ended before the British landed in Georgia and began collecting themselves. Within the next two weeks, however, a large British army was only a day's march from Charleston, and several ships blocked its harbor. The army was not yet ready to march because so many supplies had been lost at sea. And the ship captains were careful to keep their distance from the fort on Sullivan's Island that had caused them so much grief three years before. The fort was now named Fort Moultrie, for Colonel William Moultrie who had won that battle.

The Tories had fled from Charleston. The patriots who had a place to escape inland had also left. Those who remained hid in their cellars. They had already heard about the siege of Savannah. There the British shells had killed many civilians by ripping through the walls of their homes. The patriots no longer held any hope that the British would show mercy, even to women and children. During the entire march north, the invading army had destroyed homes, broken up furniture, stolen clothing, and taken every animal they could find. They forced the slaves to drive the horses and sheep with them.

When the British reached the Ashley River ferry, they began to cannonade the town. In addition to cannonballs, they fired carcases from mortars. A carcase was made of several round iron hoops, filled with explosives that started fires. In addition, pistol barrels pointing outwards were concealed in the carcase to fire balls into anyone careless enough to go near one.

The Charleston citizens had a modern fire department, with "engines," water barrels, and buckets. The engine their firemen were most proud of was a large animal bladder filled with water. One fireman carried the bladder over his shoulder, pressing on it with his arm to make it squirt out water. But when the firemen tried to put out blazes, the British soldiers shot at the firemen. As soon as a lane formed with water buckets, the British shelled the people in line. So many fires were started in the city at one time that it was impossible to put out half of them.

On April 9, 1780, the British fleet slipped past Fort Moultrie, and some ships anchored just out of reach of the guns in town. But Clinton ordered his swiftest ships to head straight for the city and turn up the Cooper River.

Through his spyglass, he had been counting the masts of several ships in the river belonging to the Americans. He had them cornered now. The prize was theirs just for the taking.

10

The Butcher Comes

THE AMERICAN ships lay at the bottom of the harbor when the British ships entered the river. Only their masts and spars showed above the water line, poised to skewer a hole through the bottom of any British ship whose captain was bold enough to advance.

Because they could not enter the Cooper River, the British could not close off the Americans' escape route through Charleston Neck and to the northward. Reinforcements continued to pour into the city by this one road. Going the other direction on the same road were soldiers, many of them friends and relatives of the Jacksons.

Five days later, hundreds of the soldiers using the escape route were surprised by "the Butcher." The Tory legion led by Lieutenant Colonel Banastre Tarleton was soon to become known all over the south, and especially to young Andrew Jackson. Tarleton was called the Butcher because of the merciless treatment of his prisoners. Soldiers who surrendered often asked for "quarter" before giving up their weapons. They were really asking for their lives to be spared in return for laying down their weapons. Tarleton promised to give quarter. Then, when the prisoners were completely helpless, the Butcher ordered his men to kill them all. "Tarleton's Quarter" became a common word for inhuman and cruel treatment of prisoners.

On May 12, the city fell to the British. One of the last to use the escape route was Colonel Thomas Sumter, with some of the Waxhaw men. General Lincoln, Major Robert Crawford, and many of the Waxhaw militia were taken prisoner by the new commander, General Lord Cornwallis.

Luckily, Cornwallis, not Tarleton, was in charge. He could not keep all five thousand of his prisoners, so he offered to release some "on parole." This meant that they must give their word of honor not to continue to fight. The Waxhaw men were only too glad to give their word and go home. Major Crawford was one of those released, but he had to leave behind his silver-mounted sword. Five hundred prisoners agreed to enlist in the British army if they were not forced to fight Americans.

Cornwallis got rid of Charleston's "Liberty Tree" at once. His men cut off its branches, piled them against the trunk, and set fire to it. But after the war was over, the undamaged tree trunk was dug out of the ground. A sculptor cut some of the wood into cane heads, and one was given to Thomas Jefferson. Some of the tree root was sliced and made into a ballot box, which was used by the South Carolinians until it burned in the courthouse fire of 1838.

Tarleton was sent out to clean up the many small groups of patriots still causing trouble in the Upcountry. The Butcher set about the task in his own bloody way. The Waxhaw country was on his list.

The Tories returned to Charleston, now that it was safe for them. They formed Tory armies that also roamed the south, searching for rebel groups. Many Waxhaw neighbors of the Jacksons were among the leaders of the rebels—Thomas Sumter, Elijah Clarke, and Andrew Pickens. They struck at British and Tory patrols, disappearing as suddenly as they had come. Francis Marion, the "Swamp Fox," was an expert at this hit-and-run game. He had been a major under Colonel Moultrie at Sullivan's Island in 1776.

Robert Crawford rode home quickly, the sweet taste of

freedom in his mouth. He cared nothing for his "gentleman's word" given to the enemy. Next time he would put his militia on horses.

Young Andrew hung around the camp constantly now. On his hat he wore a green twig, symbol of a Waxhaw militiaman. The school at Waxhaw church had ended abruptly. So had church services. As soon as the preacher, Mr. Craighead, had heard of the fall of Charleston, he had packed his bag and fled to the north. Not even Betty Jackson's pleas could keep Andrew from being a soldier now that he was thirteen.

Major Crawford had just returned from prison when his messengers told him that a small regiment of four hundred patriots was camped about ten miles from his plantation. He rode over with his men and offered to join their colonel, named Buford. They had only two field pieces and a small detachment of cavalry besides their muskets. Colonel Buford was glad for the extra hands.

The Butcher arrived one day later, on May 29, 1780.

Tarleton's Tory legion had the patriots surrounded before they knew it. He demanded Buford's immediate surrender. Buford had only a minute to consider. Tarleton could not possibly have his entire legion with him. Only two days before, Buford had had reports that the Butcher had been one hundred fifty miles to the south. Buford reasoned that if his men fought, then at least a few of them could escape. For Major Crawford, capture would mean instant death, because he had been set free on parole. Buford had no way of knowing that Tarleton really had ridden seven hundred of his men for an almost impossible fifty-four hours straight. Buford weighed the little information that he had, and refused to surrender.

Before Buford had even had time to sound a drum or give his men an order, Tarleton's men roared into the camp. Some men fired. Most threw down their arms and called for quarter, but none was given. Men with no weapons were hacked to pieces. The few who escaped fled to the Waxhaw church and gave the alarm.

Betty Jackson and Nancy Dunlap began to turn the church into a hospital. They sent wagons for the wounded. Andrew spread straw on the church floor. Rob leaped on his horse and rode to warn the neighbors. Most fled to the north with their children. But many women and old men hurried to the church with their supplies of medicine and rags for bandages. Among them were Esther Gaston, eighteen, and her married sister Martha.

In a few hours the first wagons returned with their loads. Esther's sixteen-year-old brother Joseph had been wounded in the face, and their cousin Joseph McClure limped in. Andy watched in horror as the Crawford boys were carried in— Joseph, William, and James, Jr.

From them he heard the story of what had happened. One hundred thirteen men had been massacred. One hundred fifty were so badly wounded they could not travel. Fifty-three had been taken prisoner by Tarleton. And only five of Tarleton's men had died.

The best news was that Major Robert Crawford had escaped and fled north. But Tarleton had heard the same news. He was determined that if he could not have Crawford, he would content himself with laying waste the Waxhaws. He sent his men to plunder the homes of all rebels who refused to pledge allegiance and throw themselves on the mercy of King George.

"Take every bit of food, every animal. What you cannot take, destroy!"

Tarleton's bloodthirsty men were only too happy to obey such orders. They dug up bodies that had recently been buried in family cemeteries "to see whether the family silver had been hidden in the coffin." One of the Crawford daughters was murdered with her newborn baby. Her husband, Martin McGary, wild with grief, spent the rest of his short life hunting down British redcoats and shooting them on sight.

As soon as possible, the wounded men at Waxhaw Church had to be moved. But the able-bodied men were all in the militia, and the women could not move them alone. The

faithful Catawba Indians came to the rescue, pointing out forest trails where they were safe from the redcoats and carrying the injured on their horses. The most seriously hurt were taken to Charlotte by wagon under cover of darkness.

Tarleton's legion camped about ten miles south, near the post road, until they had laid the Waxhaws bare. Once the Butcher himself was in the sights of Andy's musket. Andrew tells it, in his own handwriting:

> . . . Genl. Losley (Alexander Leslie), or Col Losley, of the British army with Infantry, & Tarlenton dragoons, advanced. The Infantry as far as Cain Creek, & Tarlton, passed thro the Waxhaw settlement to the cotauba (Catawba) nation passing our dwelling but all were *hid out*. Tarleton passed within a hundred yards of where I & a cousin crawford, had concealed ourselves. I could have shot him.

Soon thereafter, the British advanced northward once more. The three Jacksons walked to Charlotte, driving their few valuable livestock before them.

They walked down the dusty main street into the city. No sign of life showed on either side. Why so quiet? Suddenly a man stepped out from behind a wooden barricade.

"One of Sumter's men!"

He hustled the three out of sight to a cellar where they would be safe. At any minute, he explained, the British were expected to come down the same road.

But the British never came. They had pulled back.

A few days later, the Jacksons returned home. Behind them came the Carolina Gamecock, Colonel Sumter, and six hundred men. Among them was Major Robert Crawford, mounted on a three quarters blooded gelding fifteen hands high. The elite corps of the regiment, however, was made up of the new "dragoons" of Major William Richardson Davie, Andrew's old friend. Riding with the dragoons were two of Major Robert Crawford's sons, and Andrew's cousins—William, Joseph, and James Crawford, Jr.

11

The Gamecock Returns

How COULD ANDREW lie about his age to a man who remembered the day he was born?

He still had not found the answer when Major Davie rode up and swung gracefully down from his stallion. Major Crawford's military camp was busier than ever, with men rebuilding what British forage parties had tried to destroy. Andy decided to start off with a list of his qualifications.

"Sir, I am a good rider. And I know all the roads. Even many Indian paths. . . ."

Major Davie laughed and enlisted Andrew Jackson on the spot as a mounted messenger.

"I'm sure you are well fitted for the job," said the Major. "And I know how badly we need you."

He gave Andrew a pistol and showed him how to use it. Then he sent his orderly to find a proper fast horse for the new messenger.

"Not a tackie," he ordered, referring to the undesirable sort of horse that was the only kind a man could find these days. William Richardson Davie had just recruited a boy who would worship him forever.

Andrew first saw action at a place called Hanging Rock on August 6, 1780. He had delivered a message to Land's Ford on the Catawba, where several detachments met. He overheard the officers talking about an attack the next day on the British garrison near Camden, South Carolina.

"If we can clear them out at Hanging Rock, they can be made to leave their other posts nearby," said one of the captains.

". . . about five hundred men there," said another. "But that includes the Prince of Wales Regiment, some of Brown's Corps of Provincials, some legion infantry, and Colonel Bryan's North Carolina Tories."

Major Davie suggested leaving the horses some distance away from the camp and attacking on foot.

"The terrain is not good for using horses," he said. "Several large boulders, and exceptionally hard granite for them to gain a foothold."

But he was overruled by three colonels, including Sumter the Gamecock, who was in charge. Andy wished they would listen to Davie. He was much younger than the others, but he was clever.

Andy's orders were to hang back, watch the action, and be ready to ride for help in case of disaster. Next day, the column turned off the road before the enemy's picket could spot them and warn the British. The guides led them through deep woods toward the camp. But instead of landing in the center of the encampment and cutting the camp in half, they all arrived at the end where Bryan's Tories were.

The Tories ran in confusion toward the center of the camp, and the Americans were under deadly fire for awhile. At last the legion infantry gave up firing. The enemy camp seemed ready to surrender. But suddenly, just when Andrew thought the Americans had won, Brown's Corps came roaring out of the woods. They seemed to come from all directions, pouring on heavy fire as they ran.

From where Andrew watched, he thought the British had won. Then he realized he could not see a single British officer left standing. Several of the British line, however, had formed themselves into a hollow square, ready to fight to the death. The British soldiers not in the square were surrendering, asking for quarter.

The very moment of victory had come—and then, without warning, Andrew saw everything begin to fall apart. Sumter and other officers were trying to make their men attack the British square. But only Davie's men were under control. The rest of the Americans seemed suddenly to have gone berserk.

With shouts of joy they fell upon the stores. From a distance, Andy thought they must have found more soldiers hiding. But no, they were ripping open wooden boxes and turning over barrels. They had dropped their guns and, with both hands, each man was looting and grasping bottles . . . of liquor!

Deeper in the woods beyond the clearing, Andy could see flashes of movement. The legion infantry, Bryan's Tories, and Brown's regiment were starting to re-form their lines. Andrew wanted to shout, but Major Davie had noticed the same scene. Coolheaded, he collected his men. They passed around the opposite side of the scramble and melted into the woods. In a few minutes, which seemed like hours to Andrew, Davie's men fell on the British troops as they were rallying to return to the fight. They scattered and ran.

When Major Davie returned to the center of the camp, the colonels wasted a valuable hour taking the paroles of the British officers and getting litters ready for the wounded. Pushing the drunk soldiers was no easy job. Luckily, the British soldiers in the square were too far away to fire on them. They merely watched, probably enjoying the ridiculous behavior of the soldiers who had just attacked them.

Retreat was sounded now, and some of the patriots were so drunk they had to be forced to join the line. As they moved out of the woods, two British companies, which had heard shots, left the road and took position in the woods.

Major Davie spotted them and charged with his dragoons. The reinforcements disappeared farther into the woods. At last Sumter got his men into the line of march, and with Davie's men covering the rear, they returned to the Waxhaws. Andrew helped with the wounded. One of them was James Crawford, Jr.

Ten nights later, on August 16, General Gates's army was totally defeated by Cornwallis at Camden, South Carolina. That day Colonel Sumter had captured a British supply train. Then he fell back to defend the Waxhaws. He stopped at Fishing Creek to let his men rest.

The day was as hot as it gets in mid-August in South Carolina. The scene was peaceful and quiet. The colonel's and Major Crawford's horses were unsaddled and grazing nearby. A young drummer boy had stripped and jumped into the creek, and the water looked so inviting that the colonel was about to join him.

Suddenly, out of nowhere, came the Butcher, Tarleton. Sumter grabbed the drummer boy and leaped on his unsaddled horse. They galloped all the way to Charlotte before he realized he did not even have his hat. Major Crawford turned to see that his fine horse was already in enemy hands. He fled on foot, taking an Indian path he knew well. William and Joseph Crawford were taken prisoner.

Cornwallis and his men had been feeding off the Waxhaw people for a long while, foraging through the countryside. For a short time, he had moved into Robert Crawford's house, setting up his headquarters in the base camp once used by the Waxhaw militia.

Crawford gathered together the remains of Colonel Sumter's men and joined them to his own. Hard up for arms and bullets, he had his pewter dishes melted down for bullets and used the farm tools to make weapons. The wagons were gone, too. He managed to get more from his neighbor, Mr. Massey. He bought horses for them with what money he had left. Then he started "up West." Jack Sevier had once offered, for the army, the mountain men who came from beyond the Blue Ridge. If ever they were needed, it was now.

Andrew Jackson was becoming a skilled messenger and a secretive one. One day Susan Smart, a pretty fourteen-year-old, recorded in her diary meeting him along the road. She was waiting on the post road to learn some news about her father and brothers, who were with the army. A solitary lanky rider came up the road.

"Where are you from?" she asked, the way all travelers began conversations on the road.

"From below."

"Where are you going?"

"Above."

"Who are you for?" she asked him.

"The Congress."

Susan breathed a sigh of relief. The gangling redhead was so tall that his feet could reach around the belly of the tackie he was riding, but she liked his blue eyes. She asked his name.

"Andrew Jackson."

Susan told him she was also for the Congress. Then she asked for some news and told him her father was with General Gates's army. Andrew told her that Gates's army was no more.

"But we are popping them still," he said, hurrying on his way.

Major Davie had met up with Tarleton several times and had no fear of the Butcher. Once Tarleton seized the home of Captain Wachob (also spelled Walkup). He sent Wachob's wife and children to live in the cellar. But Wachob was in Davie's regiment, and soon the Butcher had company. With one quick surprise visit, Davie's men laid out sixty dead British in Wachob's front yard. Captain Wachob had just time to kiss his wife and children before he escaped with Davie's men up the road.

12

Hornet's Nest

On September 26, 1780, three Jacksons hurried once more up the post road toward Charlotte. Andrew and Rob kept looking back, but their mother's eyes were on the road straight ahead.

"On the advance of Cornwallice, we again retired," Andrew wrote in his memoirs, using the army word "retired" to mean they were retreating to the northward, "& passed charlott in Mclenburge county a few hours before the British entered it."

The eerie silence along the road gave the three a prickly feeling. The boys thought it strange they heard no horses' hooves. Even the birds in the trees made no sound.

Before they reached the courthouse, a soldier stepped out and whisked the Jacksons off the main street. From behind the scenes, Andy had just time for a quick look at the surprise waiting for Cornwallis. Davie, now a colonel at twenty-four, had placed twenty of his best men behind a stone wall under the courthouse steps. Other companies had been stationed behind houses.

The main force of the army under Sumter had retreated to Salisbury. Davie's orders were to delay Cornwallis at Charlotte as long as possible. A few hours later the British rode into the trap, completely unaware. Finally, with a flanking movement, they forced Davie to retreat. But he had delayed the

British advance by a whole day. And Charlotte earned the name Cornwallis gave it—"the Hornet's Nest."

Betty Jackson and Robert had continued their long flight before the battle began. But Andrew had been left in Charlotte to stay with Mrs. Wilson, a sister of his Uncle George McKemey, and his cousin John Wilson. He heard every whizzing bullet and the horses' hooves outside, but he saw nothing, because Mrs. Wilson made him stay in the cellar with her family.

Andrew suspected his mother might have had another reason for leaving him to get acquainted with his cousin John Wilson, who was about his age. John was going to be a minister. He was as different from Andrew as it was possible to be. The visit was a painful one for John. He said later that he had never heard such language or seen a boy show off his deadly weapons with such glee. Over forty years later, when Andrew Jackson ran for president, his disgusted cousin did not vote for him.

In October, the men that Major Crawford had ridden up west to find came down out of the mountains. Jack Sevier and one thousand men, who were dressed and fought more like Indians than soldiers, arrived at Sycamore Shoals on their way to Kings Mountain. They were joined by militia from Virginia and South Carolina, including Major Crawford and his Waxhaw men.

The target was a British leader as cruel and ruthless as Tarleton. He was Major Patrick Ferguson. Ferguson's troops had camped on the bald top of King's Mountain, heavily forested with trees on all sides.

"That set of mongrels," Ferguson had called the mountain men, when he heard they were marching toward him through pouring rain. "If they rise up, I'll hang their leaders and lay their country waste with fire and sword."

The Americans surrounded the hill as soon as the rain stopped, on October 7, 1780. The leaders told the mountain men not to wait for a word of command, but to follow their leaders and fire as quickly as possible. Any who were afraid were invited to take themselves off immediately.

"Here I would willingly have been excused," said one boy of sixteen, "but I could not well swallow the name of coward."

Every man put four or five balls in his mouth "to prevent thirst," and also to be ready to reload fast. They climbed the hill, were repulsed, climbed again, fell back, and went up a third time. By then they realized that, while all their shots were hitting the mark, the British shooting downward were not having the same luck. Their bullets were passing just above the heads of the mountain men.

The battle was over in an hour. Ferguson was dead, and seven hundred were prisoners. The mountain men, satisfied they had done a good job, headed back to the hills.

One week later, Cornwallis began his retreat back to South Carolina. The rain did not let up for days. The British were in mud over their boots. Often they were without food, mainly because they had already destroyed everything in their path on the march north.

Francis Marion, the Swamp Fox, and Colonel Sumter's men added to the British discomforts with as many more stings as they could inflict. Marion had a very efficient spy network, even in Charleston under the very noses of the redcoats.

One of the "spies" was a very small boy named George Spidel. George was an apprentice to Captain Bellamy and lived at his home in Charleston. But George's duties often included going on trading expeditions with Joshua Lockwood in his small boat. Lockwood guided his craft skillfully through creeks and inland marshes, stopping at various landings.

When they landed, small George delivered a bundle to a family, or sometimes Captain Bellamy gave him a basket with small articles to sell. Lockwood always told him which house he must go to first. Then he must continue to sell more articles from the basket to avoid suspicion.

Once a Tory suspected him, but George pretended to be childish, and they let him go. Another time, when Lockwood landed his boat back in Charleston, some Tories were waiting at the dock. Two grabbed Lockwood, and another searched the boat. George heard the commotion from his hiding place and knew he must pretend he had run away from his master, Captain Bellamy. The Tories found him, and led him to Bellamy's house. The captain pretended to be very angry.

"That boy must be punished," he fumed. "He is always running away."

He thanked the Tories for finding him and gave them a reward. Then he yanked George in the door roughly, closed it, and gave the weeping boy a hug.

During the winter, General Nathanael Greene took over the southern army. One month later, on January 17, 1781, Tarleton the Butcher was badly defeated in a battle fought at the Cowpens. And in March, Cornwallis had to change his plans completely after a battle at Guilford Court House.

Just before Tarleton's defeat, Colonel "Lighthorse Harry" Lee had played a trick on the British that put huge smiles on all the patriots' faces. Lee had tricked two Tory riders into believing that he was Tarleton. They led Lee and his men back to a British column of four hundred men. Straight between the rows of redcoats they marched, and captured or killed the entire force without losing a single man.

The war was going so well that it was easy to be overconfident. One night Andy and Rob Jackson were sleeping blissfully at Major Crawford's headquarters at Land's Ford. Only one man was awake. He leaped up suddenly, grabbing Andy by the hair.

"The Tories are upon us!"

Andy grabbed a short-barreled musket that was loaded with buckshot for short range. It was so heavy he had to support it in the fork of a tree. He fired at figures hiding in the shadows. The man who had wakened him was killed. Andy ran for the house. He and six others began firing out of the windows. James Crawford, probably the son of the Major, was hit.

"They're coming in," one of the men shouted. Andy counted

many more Tories than they could handle. Then suddenly came the sound of a bugle.

Cavalry charge! The Tories dashed for their horses and rode off into the forest. The woods were silent as death. Where was the sound of cavalry horses? Andy risked putting his face in the window. Standing in the clearing was one man, Mr. Isabel, holding a bugle.

The next time the Tories came to the Waxhaws, they were not alone. Major Crawford was holding a meeting at the Waxhaw church on April 9 when the picket saw a small group of men in country clothes coming toward them.

"Reinforcements under Captain Nesbit," thought the guard.

But as they came closer, there seemed to be more. Suddenly the "country people" turned aside. Behind them was a company of Tory dragoons under Major Coffin, with sabers drawn. While one group charged the meetinghouse, the country people dismounted. Another group of dragoons charged on horse.

Andrew Jackson leaped out a window and onto his horse in an instant. Lieutenant Thomas Crawford also managed to ride off, but with a dragoon in hot pursuit.

"Follow me," Andrew called to Thomas.

Now was the time to find again the swampy path he had often ridden on the way to school at the meetinghouse. Andy headed for the only place he knew where Cain Creek had a rocky bottom. He crossed in safety, but Thomas's horse had mired. The dragoon fired, and Thomas was injured. He was taken prisoner.

Andrew rode on sadly to a spot he knew was high enough to let him spend the night. Near dusk, another figure on horseback came across the swamp. It was Rob. Next morning the two boys were hungry, and Andy was curious to know what had happened to Major Crawford's son Thomas.

Watching and listening carefully the whole way, they rode to Thomas Crawford's house. A Tory neighbor saw them. Before they had finished breakfast, a file of dragoons burst in the door.

"Hiding rebels!" the dragoons shouted, and began smashing everything in the house. Andy and Rob could do nothing to help the family. One of the officers was the man who had chased them into the swamp the day before.

"Clean my boots," he ordered Andy. But Andy refused, saying he was a prisoner of war and expected to be treated like one.

The officer was in an ugly enough mood without a sassy redhead answering back. He lifted his saber and brought it down hard toward Andy's head. Andy's left arm shot up and broke some of the force, but he knew the sword had hit bone. A gash on his head from the point of the sword bled heavily into his eye. Rob moved to defend his brother, and he too was cut by the saber.

The officer sent Rob out and ordered Andy to mount a horse and lead him to a rebel, Major Thompson, who had escaped the day before.

"I'll kill you straight off, if you don't," he warned.

Andy started off toward Thompson's house, almost blinded by the blood in his eye. He knew two ways to get to Thompson's. A path through the woods was the quickest. But he led the dragoons through an open field. That way Thompson could see them coming from half a mile away. By the time the soldiers reached his door, he had leaped onto his horse, swum across a swollen creek, and escaped.

Andy and Rob were not so lucky. They were forced to march, separately, so they could not see each other. Without food, water, or even a bandage, they were taken to Camden jail, forty miles away.

Andy was put on the second floor of the jailhouse, in the British camp commanded by Lord Francis Rawdon.

"My boy can use these," said a Tory, stealing Andy's coat and shoes.

Almost all Andrew's fellow prisoners were too sick or badly wounded to take pity on a boy of fourteen. "I frequently heard them groaning in the agonies of death, and no regard was paid to them," Andrew told friends years later. He found a place by a north-facing window where the air smelled a little less foul, and the prisoners gave him his ration of one piece of stale bread each day. His own wounds received no treatment at all, and he knew only that his head and fingers would heal better if he could "get all the bad blood out" by encouraging them to bleed.

From his window seat a few days later, Andrew saw the American army under General Greene a mile away on Hobkirk's Hill.

"They've got no guns," one of the Tory guards told the prisoners. "We're going to make a second Gates out of him, and then hang all of you."

On April 25, Andrew saw an American soldier approach Lord Rawdon's headquarters. He supposed it was a deserter or a spy. Shortly after, the prisoners noticed a stir through the British camp. Just before sundown, soldiers came into their prison room and nailed boards across the window. The able guards were replaced by Tories who had been wounded and were no longer able to fight. Obviously, a battle was planned.

None of the prisoners wanted to miss seeing the action. Andrew suggested he use their one razor blade, saved for cutting up their rations, to scratch out a knothole in the boarded-up window. All night he worked at it, finally getting one hole just large enough for his eye.

The British attack on Greene's position was such a surprise to the Americans that many of them were half dressed. Several officers were washing their feet, and soldiers were washing out their kettles after breakfast. But they formed their lines at once.

The British officers told their men the Americans had no artillery. They, as well as the prisoners back in the jailhouse, were surprised when Greene's battery opened on them. Cheers and huzzahs from the prisoners sounded each time Andy reported good news seen through his knothole. The British were confused and running helter-skelter. But the battle was not over.

"How short was our Joy," Andrew Jackson said many years later. "Soon thereafter the roar of the cannon ceased . . . the sound of our small arms appeared retiring. . . ."

A new prisoner, Captain Smith, was shoved roughly into the room, wearing only shorts and drawers. He had not had time to dress, the attack had come so fast. He filled in the prisoners on the parts of the battle that Andy could not see.

A few days after the battle, help came from an unexpected source.

Betty Jackson visited Lord Rawdon. She had heard there was to be an exchange of prisoners, and she asked that her two boys be among them. Lord Rawdon was impressed with this small gutsy redheaded woman who loved her sons enough to walk into the enemy camp.

13

Alone at Sixteen

"JACKSON?" CALLED a rough voice as the metal door scraped open.

Andrew got up slowly. The fever was on him, and for the first unsteady moments on his feet, he thought he might have imagined he heard his name called. But it was true. The Tory was holding the door open and motioning for him. Slamming it again, he pointed down the steps.

Betty Jackson stood at the outside door, holding two sad-looking tackies. Andrew was bareheaded and barefooted, and had no coat. But the rush of fresh spring air, still filled with the smell of gunpowder from the battle, erased the stench of the prison he had left behind.

Then, with horror, he saw his brother Rob led out. Rob's face was covered with smallpox, and his head wound was running with pus. They helped him onto one of the tackies, but he could not stay up without being held by one of the other men who was being exchanged.

Mrs. Jackson rode the other horse while Andrew walked. She could not lead her family away from Camden fast enough and started for the post road. But Andrew, revived somewhat by the cool air, begged to pass by Hobkirk's Hill.

"I traversed the battle ground," Andrew told his friends

later, "found many musquets without their locks, with their Bayonets stuck in the earth with their butts up, & some barrells out of their stocks, every appearance indicated a sudden unexpected attack & when they were cleaning their arms."

The trip home was agony. Many years later the grim details were still vivid in Andrew Jackson's memory.

"Having only two horses in our company when we left Camden, and my brother, on account of weakness caused by a severe bowel complaint and the wound he had received on his head, being obliged to be held on the horse, and my mother riding the other, I was compelled to walk the whole way.

"The distance to the nearest house . . . where we stopped that night was forty-five miles and the enemy having taken my shoes and jacket I had to trudge along barefooted. The fury of a violent storm of rain to which we were exposed for several hours before we reached the end of our journey caused the small pox to strike in and consequently the next day I was dangerously ill. . . ."

Rob died two days later, just as they reached home. Betty had no time to grieve. Her only son was now close to death because the pox had struck. With the help of friends who had already had the disease, she worked at raising a fever that would bring the smallpox out. Pockmarks were ugly, but at least he could survive.

At last Andrew, barely conscious through it all, had a high fever and the pox came out. He was out of danger. But he looked like a skeleton with steely blue eyes.

The sickness left Andrew as weak as a newborn babe. His mother nursed him through the long summer, keeping his spirits up with conversation about their friends and relatives. Andy and his brothers had heard her tell many times about the suffering of their grandfather at the siege of Carrickfergus, when the Irish lords had made the poor Scottish peasants suffer. But this time, Andrew understood suffering. How his grandfather must have hated the Irish! Just so, Andrew would carry a lifelong hatred of the British redcoat.

Mrs. Jackson tried to answer all his questions about the Waxhaw militia. The men who had not been captured or killed had packed up their families and moved to a safer part of the country. Their meeting place at the Waxhaw church had been burned down by the dragoons after Andy and Rob had been led away, and had not been rebuilt.

Colonel Davie and his men of horse still roamed the countryside, but Major Robert Crawford no longer had an army. Without men, he could not command a regiment and keep his rank as a major. Like many of those fighting for independence, he had never really been a part of the Continental Army. His wife was about to have their eighth child, but Crawford was determined to fight to the bitter end. At the age of fifty-three, he became a private and a wagoner. Then he joined Francis Marion, the Swamp Fox, and became his aide.

Nancy Richardson Dunlap, Betty's good friend, came one day to cheer Andy. Even she had a war story to tell. She had gone to visit her sister Rachel in Guilford, North Carolina. When Rachel's preacher husband, Dr. Caldwell, came home for a visit, the house was surrounded by armed Tories. They were going to take him to the British camp.

While two of the men guarded Dr. Caldwell, the others plundered the house. When they had collected everything they wanted, they dumped their treasures in the middle of the floor.

Nancy Dunlap stood behind Dr. Caldwell and whispered into his ear, as if she had intended only him to hear.

"Isn't it time for Gillespie and his men to get here?"

One of the soldiers overheard, just as she had intended.

"What men?" he asked in alarm.

"I was talking only to my brother," Nancy snapped. Suddenly the Tories panicked. The name of the rebel Gillespie was terrifying to Tories. The men left hurriedly, leaving behind both the prisoner and the loot.

These stories of his home country and the people who made

up his world helped Andrew to find himself again. And though nothing would ever be the same without Hugh and Rob, he began to see that life was still worth living. Besides, he owed his mother a duty not to leave her alone.

News of the war was getting much brighter. The British had now lost all their inland forts in the Carolinas. They controlled only Charleston and Savannah, because of the British ships anchored in the harbors. Cornwallis had headed toward Virginia. He could succeed in cutting the colonies in half. Andrew had seen some bloody sights in the war. Now he wanted very much to live long enough to see the British beaten.

Summer's hot days at last began to yield to cooler nights. Andrew was much stronger by September, and Mrs. Jackson's mind turned to one more duty she must perform. She had promised her dying sister, Jennet Crawford, that she would care for the younger boys, Joseph and William. Both boys had been taken prisoner. Now Betty learned from Nancy Dunlap where they were being held.

They were in a prison ship in Charleston harbor, Nancy told her. The women could imagine what horrors their men had gone through—confined in the hold of a ship through the heat of the past summer.

Nancy Dunlap and a Mrs. Boyd were going to visit the prison ship. If they could not get the younger prisoners re-leased, then at least they might be permitted to nurse the sick ones.

"I'll go with you," Betty Jackson said, almost without hesitation.

She packed a small bundle with a change of clothes and gathered what few medicines and herbs she had left. She did not kiss Andrew. He was, after all his experiences, a man now. But there was always a chance she would not return. She stammered a little, trying to find just the right words to say.

Andrew wished for the rest of his life that he could re-member her words exactly. But he could not. He recalled only that she wanted to leave him with a few words of "mother's advice." Later it came back to him in bits and pieces.

"Andrew, make your friends by being honest . . . keep them by being steadfast. Never tell a lie . . . nor take what is not your own . . . nor sue for slander. . . . Settle them cases yourself."

Andrew watched his mother and the others start once more down the long road to Charleston. From the set of her chin, he knew that she would find his Crawford cousins. He took some pleasure in imagining how surprised Joseph and William would be when she bent over them. He knew that he would never forget his surprise when she showed up at the Camden prison to take Rob and him home.

The story of what happened to Betty Jackson after she walked down the post road to Charleston comes from many different sources. The ladies stopped in Charleston at the home of Mrs. Agnes Barton, about a mile from the "Governor's Gate." Since the governors in the early days lived at *Belvedere*, this gate may have been at the entrance road to that plantation.

When the ladies reached the prison ship, Betty Jackson found Joseph Crawford dying of smallpox. She nursed him but could not save him. She did manage to free William Crawford. The war changed drastically in mid-October, 1781, when Cornwallis was forced to surrender to General Washington in Yorktown. Perhaps that surrender helped set William free.

Nothing, however, could help Betty Jackson. She came down with smallpox and died in November at the Bartons' house. Nancy Dunlap and Mrs. Boyd were with her. Mrs. Barton told Andrew many years later that her husband had made the coffin. Betty Jackson was buried in an unmarked grave near the Bartons' house, and Andrew was never able to find her.

Nancy Dunlap carried home the small bundle of Betty's spare clothing and handed it sadly to Andrew. Not many words were spoken. He remembered his mother saying that only girls were made for crying.

Andrew Jackson felt utterly alone.

The end of the war did not bring the joy Andrew and the others in the Waxhaws had expected to feel—only poverty and problems. After seven years of service, Major Robert Crawford sent his bill to the new government to get back some of the money he had laid out for his militia. William Crawford, home from the prison ship, asked Andrew to appraise the horse he had lost when he was captured.

"One hundred fifty pounds," Andrew decided. William hoped he would get it.

Andrew stayed for a while with his Aunt Margaret and Uncle George McKemey. Then he moved to Major Crawford's. Andrew liked being around horses, and for a short time he was apprenticed to a saddler. Fevers and "the shakes" still plagued him. He thought a little of moving up West, where many of the poor Waxhaw people had gone.

One day Andrew rode his uncle's tackie over to the farm his father had bought before he was born. Andrew now owned the whole two hundred acres of red soil, trees, and swamp. The land was poor for farming, and he had no desire to farm anyway. It was not even good land for raising cattle, as Major Crawford had done in the old days. Andrew might try breeding horses, but he had no money. A good blooded horse cost a great deal of money, and nobody wanted to buy little grass ponies any more. He had no idea what to do.

Help came from a completely unexpected source. The grandfather he had never known, except through his mother's stories, died in Ireland. He had left an unknown sum of money to his grandsons, and now only Andrew was alive to claim it.

Andrew was sixteen in 1783 when the British finally left the city they still called Charles Town and the Americans were now calling Charleston. He rode into town and stopped at the Quarter House Tavern. There an attorney for his grandfather handed him his inheritance.

14

Lubber in Finery

"ALMOST FOUR hundred pounds!" Andrew gasped.

To him it seemed a fortune that would never run out. He could buy land, or blooded race horses, or even a carriage left behind by some fleeing Tory.

His first stop was for some grand clothes. Unlike the Waxhaws, where no one had ever been able to buy anything luxurious, Charleston was filled with comforts for the gentry. Silver tea sets and porcelain cups as delicate as eggshells were displayed for sale in shop windows. Andy knew families in the Waxhaws that had buried such valuable items in their family cemeteries to keep the British and Tories from stealing them, but he knew of no one who had beautiful things like that in their homes where they could be used.

Next he bought a good-looking horse. She was no *Roebuck* like the horse owned by Captain James, a scout for the Swamp Fox, but Andrew Jackson knew horseflesh. The British had brought fine horses from England for their dragoons and had not been able to take them home again.

Andrew rode his new mare proudly around the city and left his card at the homes of some of the young men he had met at the Cummins school. He located many of them, and found them to be as bored as he was with a life of peace. The carefully reared young men of Charleston were fascinated by Jackson, a soldier scarred in the service of his country—a "rustic" with what appeared to be an unending supply of money. What sport!

If they were intrigued by Andrew, he was just as impressed with them. He was hypnotized by their lazy lifestyle. Invited to their homes for dinner, Andy found the table surrounded by servants. A slave was called for the least job—butter my bread, cut my beef, move my chair to the left.

On the city streets, Andrew saw tradesmen walking along the brick sidewalks, slaves directly behind them carrying their tools. When one of his new friends suggested that he go to a barber and "get his head adjusted," he found the barber visiting with his customers while the black slave did his work. Most of his friends' fathers were "planters." They had country plantations but knew nothing about planting. Their overseers did all the work.

Andy had only one thing in common with his old friends— boredom. They had all had adventures during the war, although several of the Charleston boys had been officers. Now the excitement was over, and they had no idea what to do next.

One was going to be a lawyer. His diary gives an idea of how hard he was working at that:

"Just come home to dinner," he writes. "I have not done as much as I ought to have done. I read some. Should have finished. It would have been better than losing three out of four games at billiards."

Many of the boys were being pushed into early marriages, arranged by their parents between cousins in order to keep their large plantations within the family.

"Had a discharge of guns to celebrate my friend's marriage," one boy wrote. "I hear she did not want to marry him. Hope it is not true the parents forced the match. . . . Received a kind invitation to dine with the groom tomorrow. Many gents were there to eat a Wedding Dinner with him. It was not much like one though, as there was no Bride at table."

One day Andrew was delighted with the aimless rich life

led by his friends; the next day he was disgusted with their laziness. He realized soon after he paid his first bills in Charleston that he was going to have to find more money to keep up with their fast pace. He could take care of that by gambling and winning at the horse races.

Charleston was a far lovelier city than Andrew Jackson had remembered it as a cattledriver five years before. It had not suffered from British occupation. Many public squares planted with trees and flowers kept the air fresh and cool. The streets were straight, but much narrower than the post road. They were sandy, so that rumbling carriage wheels made hardly a sound going by. People on foot used the wide brick sidewalks. Only crossing the street was disagreeable—the sand made Andrew's new shoes dusty.

Most of the buildings were brick and one story high. None were higher than three stories. But all the houses faced onto gardens. No main doorway was on the street side of the house.

Fire, the greatest danger in cities, was controlled by thirteen wardens. Each kept five hogsheads, large barrels strongly made and filled with water. In case of alarm, all sixty-five hogsheads of water were to be rolled to the scene of the fire at once.

Sometimes Andy met his friends' sisters, but usually those of marriageable age were kept far away from someone considered as unsuitable as Andrew Jackson. No matter, he shrugged. If the belles of Charleston would not have him, he would have the kind of girl he could buy.

"A stranger meets a female by slow degrees," a friend told him, "interspersed with little niceties." The young ladies were not much fun anyway, because they had been taught not to be forward. Andrew found the gentlemen much more sociable, although he thought they drank too much.

He was a graceful figure on the ballroom floor, after some quick private lessons in dancing. Balls in Charleston began at six in the evening and ended during the wee hours of the morning. The ladies had their hair dressed so high that most looked taller than Andrew, with ribbons and even fake birds tucked into their curls. Their dresses had so much whalebone sewed into the seams that the boys called them "ironclads." But Jackson could not help admiring the men. Each one who had been a military officer wore his sword.

Men also wore their swords to some concerts. Although Andrew did not enjoy sitting still and listening to music, he did like going to the St. Cecilia Society, where only the cream of society was invited.

Some of Andrew Jackson's friends also invited him to their plantations when the weather was cool. They told him it was almost vulgar to spend a holiday in the city. In the country, life was far less formal. There, the ladies who were so cool in the drawing room were like birds uncaged. When the young men went hunting, the ladies beat the bushes to stir up small game. On a rice plantation, the girls climbed up the rice stacks and perched on top.

"Then the gents climb up too, the rice collapses, and they all ride down," one of the young men told Andy.

One day his friends formed a "maroon party." Going marooning meant to go off alone. That time they went to visit a sawmill—no great adventure for Andy, who had already seen several. Evidently it was a lark for his city-bound friends, who seldom strayed away from the safety of their small world. They had a word for the country people that offended Andy, but he laughed with the rest of them at the "lubbers" who showed them around the sawmill.

Lubbers had no voice in the government, one of the boys told Andy. Only the large plantation owners had had seats in the old Assembly. They hoped to go on making all the laws now under the new government.

One maroon party turned out to be dinner under the trees in the country. This, too, was no great adventure to an ex-soldier. While they were eating, a gentleman came down the road. To Andy he appeared by his clothing, his haughty air, and the goodness of his horse to be someone of distinction.

"He cannot be a gentleman," said one of Andy's new friends.

Andy looked surprised. "Why not?"

"He's riding without a servant," said the friend.

Andy flushed. He also rode without a servant. A nagging thought entered his busy head. What did they really think of him? Were they really his friends? Then the fleeting thought was gone. They were off to try one of Andy's favorite sports—the races.

The racing season did not begin until the cool weather. Many of the boys' families had racing paths at their plantations. But for the Newmarket Races, they went to the public track. They did not go alone. The courts adjourned, schools were let out, and shops closed. No one in Charleston missed race days.

The war was one reason the horse races were so popular and necessary. The best horses had always been imported from England, but many excellent horses had been lost in battle. America could not exist without cavalry horses for its army. Racing horses was one way to determine which were the strongest and best. Then those horses would be bred to begin new breeds of American horses.

Andrew Jackson loved a good horse. He had never forgotten the beautiful horse he had seen Major Crawford riding out of Charlotte that day. He had even made bets between friends in the Waxhaws on the outcome of some impromptu horse races. But then he had won only a new hat, a pair of boots, and once a bugle. In Charleston, immediately after the race was run, a winning bettor filled his pockets with hard money!

At the paddock, young Jackson examined the racing horses carefully. He knew he should look for a horse with a light but muscular neck, one with the wide forehead that indicated a good-sized brain. Ears not too small, nostrils large, legs strong, hair thin and silky—all were signs of a horse that might win a race. Perhaps because the horses he was used to meeting in the Waxhaws were not thoroughbreds, Andy turned out not to be a good chooser of winners. At any rate, he lost a great deal of his money at the racetrack.

Andrew entertained his new friends with horse stories he had heard during the war. One mare named Red Doe had belonged to a British officer who had ridden her to the exe-

cution of an American soldier named Hunter. Hunter asked
the officer to dismount, indicating that he had something
important to say for his ears only. The instant the officer's
feet hit the ground, he felt his horse move. On her back was
Hunter, who escaped into a nearby thicket before the firing
squad knew what had happened.

The Charleston racetrack was not the only place Andrew
lost money. He gambled on everything. Although his new
friends found cockfighting beneath their dignity ("We saw the
dregs of the world at the cockfights"), they also gambled with
dice, card games, target contests, the election, lotteries, and
even next week's weather.

The money had to run out. One day Andy discovered he
owed everyone. He sold what he could part with to pay the
landlord's bill. Then, just one more bet . . . just so he could
go home with something in his pocket.

The game was rattle and roll. Andy threw the dice. On his
silent lips was probably the first prayer he had uttered in years.
The dice stopped rolling, and he could hardly believe his eyes.
He had lost. There was nothing left to part with but his new
horse. That was like losing an arm or leg. Before he let go of
the bridle, he asked for one more chance.

"My horse," he said quietly.

He knew he was talking to another gambler, like himself,
who could not resist a bet. He warmed the dice in his moist
hand. If he won, he promised himself he would leave town
fast. Then he threw the dice out on the table.

Andrew Jackson left Charleston riding his chestnut mare,
his pockets empty. Thank you, grandfather, he murmured to
himself. He had loved every minute of spending his inheritance. But perhaps his old Scottish grandfather's spirit had
been hovering around him the past few weeks. Andy had
learned a painful lesson, made friends, and lost them as quickly
as he had lost his money. His future lay up west. The Charleston gentlemen were really not his kind of people after all.

15

Upwest Rebel

ANDREW JACKSON had three days to think on the long road home from Charleston. But he was surprised at what he was thinking about.

In all his days of playing the wealthy dandy in the big city, he had hardly given a thought to the bright, laughing eyes of Mary Crawford. Now he could not get them out of his mind.

Why he should suddenly spur on his horse in the hopes of seeing Mary was a mystery to Andy. He had grown up with her, enjoyed being with her, and showed off a bit when he knew her eyes were on him. But he had never thought of her as someone to love, until the ride back from Charleston.

Mary, the daughter of Major Robert Crawford, was three months younger than Andy. They had often shared secret joys and despairs. He knew Mary liked him. Her father had not allowed her to visit him when he had the smallpox, but she had talked her parents into letting Andy stay at the Crawford home for a short while after his mother died.

His stay with the Crawfords might have been longer if he had not let his temper get the better of him. A Scottish friend of the Major's, one Captain Galbraith, was also staying there. The captain also liked the eyes of Miss Mary.

One day Andy made fun of the captain's Scottish accent. The man, who was as short of temper as Andy, had snatched up a horsewhip. Coming at Andy, he vowed he would teach him a lesson.

"I immediately answered," Jackson recalled many years later, *"that I had arrived at the age to know my rights, and although weak and feeble from disease, I had courage to defend them, and if he attempted anything of that kind I would most assuredly Send him to the other world."*

Andy had fully intended a duel to the death, but the major stepped in and settled matters quickly. He sent Andy off to visit Mr. Joseph White, an uncle of Mrs. Crawford. White's son had just started in the saddle-making business. But that career had ended when Andy learned he had inherited money from his grandfather.

What to do now? Andy had lost all his money, but he knew he would never lose the feeling he had when there was money in the leather purse tucked under his belt. He could not ask for Mary Crawford's hand in marriage until he had some land, money, and a respectable job. So far he had only the land.

Major Crawford suggested he go to the school in Charlotte, now called Liberty Hall. Colonel Davie had gone there before attending Princeton, and he had now become a lawyer. Davie had been Andrew's hero as far back as he could remember. He saw no reason to stop following in his tracks now. Lawyers were respected—and Andrew had seen several rich lawyers in Charleston.

How long Jackson stayed at Liberty Hall is unknown. After what he had been through, he was no longer schoolboy material. For a short time, he taught school near the Waxhaws. Some days he and Mary walked along the banks of the Catawba River holding hands and planning a future that never happened.

Major Crawford had many doubts about young Andrew Jackson as a son-in-law. The boy had little in his favor, except that he had survived smallpox, the war, and a serious wound.

He would most likely not die young. A father had to consider such things, because he did not want his daughter left a widow with eight or ten children to raise. But Andy was dangerously hotheaded. There were rumors of wild behavior, and heavy drinking. And by now, most people in the Waxhaws had heard how he had gambled away his inheritance of four hundred pounds in Charleston. The major had a long talk with his daughter.

Some time before December 1784, Andrew and Mary had their long talk by the river. She gave him hope that she still had deep feeling for him, and he knew how he felt about her. But a girl younger than twenty-one could not marry without her father's permission.

On December 4, Andy appraised "a Bay horse of James Crawford Lost in the Service of the State," so his cousin could get money from the new government. Then he turned his horse north on the post road and left the Waxhaws forever.

He was not alone on the road. Almost as many wagons were heading up west as Andy's parents had met coming down the Great Wagon Road twenty years before. Most were young families and single men whose homes had been burned down, their cattle and crops stolen by retreating British soldiers. Now they were heading for new country beyond the mountains.

Andrew may even have passed the peddler John Graham, whose wagon often broke down on the road between Charlotte and Salisbury. Graham had been traveling the road, with two horses pulling his movable shop, since the war ended. He drove from Charlotte, buying and selling his wares all the way north to Philadelphia and back again.

In his small notebook Graham wrote down everything he must remember to buy on a trip north:

3 pair silver buckles	1 ream good writeing paper
1 doz. linnen handker-chiefs	Black tafety bonnet with trimmings
Red durant for petti-coats	3 bibles
1 dozen knifes and forks	1 lb. pepper, 4 lb. coffee

Then he wrote down special items for certain people along his route.

> "For Sally Thompson: 1 womans rideing whip horn handel silver mounted."
> "For Isaac Alexander: One wide mouth bottle holding 1 quart and some tin foil."
> "For Capt. James Alexander: 1 ryfal gun [rifle] gun 3 feet 7 inches long. Light and handy."
> "For Jean Semple [who evidently had a death in her family] black and blue crepe, black persian, black ferritan, 3 knifes and forks, 1 pair black gloves."

Money was Graham's biggest problem. Some states issued money of their own that could not be used in other states. In addition to English pounds and shillings, people paid with Spanish dollars, French money, and Portuguese coins.

Mrs. Semple handed Graham a one-pound bill and eight shillings to pay for her articles. But country people would not accept paper money. So the peddler had to go to Dr. Noonan to change the bill into "silver." The doctor, who traveled often, was glad to have lightweight paper money to carry instead of hard money. From another customer, Graham received sixteen half "Joes." A Joe (short for "johannes") was Portuguese money, and some country people would not take that.

Peddler Graham also ran an information service. One customer planned to go into the business of making potash. Would Mr. Graham kindly ask in every city the different ways to make potash? And please purchase for him two kettles, each holding one hundred gallons, as well as two ladles to stir the liquid.

Peddlers were always looking for items that were sure-fire sellers. Graham liked selling pink root. It grew in South Carolina, took up very little space in his wagon, and sold for high prices. The doctors on his list bought all the pink root he could produce. They prescribed it to their patients to get rid of worms. Worms were a common complaint. No one knew that people had worms because they ate meat and other food with worms in it. One silversmith bought seven pounds of pink root from Graham, and paid him with silver shoe buckles, knee buckles, a watch chain, a pair of locket buttons, and a brooch "set with stone."

When Andrew saw a peddler along the road, he remembered how happy his mother had been when peddlers bought her woven goods. He recalled the smile on her face when she had coins to jingle in her apron pocket. He might have been angry if he had known how many coins the same peddler had jingling in his own pocket after he sold Betty's linen and heddie-yarn in the city.

John Graham bought furs in Carolina from several boys along his route. On one trip north he carried along forty-five raccoons, thirteen foxes, and two wildcats. He paid each boy one shilling for a raccoon or a fox, and two shillings for a cat. The country boys were thrilled to make so much money. But in Philadelphia, where wild animals were harder to find, John Graham sold the raccoon and the wildcat skins for 40 shillings each, and the fox skins for 60 shillings each.

Andrew Jackson rode into Salisbury determined to make his fortune as soon after he reached eighteen as possible. The houses were smaller and less attractive than those in Charleston, but he was impressed with the huge county courthouse. The town had a grim prison and an armory, left over from the Revolution. Along the main street were several shops and taverns.

Four shillings a day for the Rowan House seemed dear, but he had letters of introduction to a few important lawyers, and he had learned in Charleston that it was important to look successful, even though his belly might be empty.

16

Backwoods Justice

"WHEN YOU HAVE learned everything in all those books,"
Spruce Macay told Andrew, "you will be a lawyer."

Macay's bookshelves groaned with the heaviest and fattest
books Andrew had ever seen, and he groaned with them.
Macay had just agreed to take him on as an apprentice to
learn law. Another apprentice, named John McNairy, worked
for the lawyer.

McNairy was slightly more encouraging.

"You will learn much of that by just keeping your ears open
when court starts again in January," he said. "Besides, all the
effort is worthwhile, when you get your license saying you
have lived in the state two years and are a person of unblemished moral character!"

McNairy took Andrew around to Mr. Hughes's house, where
he found a room to live in for a much better price than the
Rowan House. He also arranged for Andrew to be invited to
the Christmas ball, one of Salisbury society's big events.

Andrew bought a supply of the best clothes he could find
from the only tailor who would give him credit. Clothes gave
him a confidence that he did not feel when he looked in the
mirror at his pock-marked face and the scar on his forehead
that still turned red when he was angered.

The ball was all McNairy had said it would be. When Andrew entered, his tall lean figure made heads turn. Mothers asked who he was and where he came from. The young ladies did not care. They sent their brothers over to bring him around for an introduction.

When one of the ladies turned her full artillery of charms on Andrew, as he said later to McNairy, he felt a little twisted by her. They compared notes on which ladies were handsome and which ones talked much without saying anything. But secretly, Andy thought to himself, he would not have given a snap for the whole lot of them. Shallow emptyheaded girls did not appeal to him.

When court opened in January, Andrew was amazed at the change in the small town. Taverns filled up overnight, with lawyers as well as clients who had come for justice. On the courthouse green and behind the taverns, men met in contests of strength, cockfights, wrestling, footraces, horseshoe pitching, and bowling. People had their pockets picked clean, even while they were sitting in court.

As for the study of law, one man who knew Macay said that Andrew Jackson was "the head of the rowdies . . . he's more in the stable than the office." According to Mama Judie, Macay's slave, "Never saw him study. All I ever saw him do was clean his pistols, fight cocks, and chase yellow women." Nancy Jarret, who lived in Salisbury, remembered Andy more kindly.

"We all knew he was wild," she said years later. "That he gambled and was by no means a Christian young man. Nevertheless there was something about him I cannot describe, except to say that it was a presence."

The second year, Andy's "presence" suffered a downfall. He was the manager of the Christmas ball. The evening went off perfectly, until two women of very doubtful reputation arrived at the door. Andy had sent them an invitation as a joke, never dreaming they would really show up. The women left the party, but after that nice people kept their daughters far away from Andy. His boss, Spruce Macay, was furious.

Very soon after, Colonel John Stokes took Andrew into his law office. Stokes had lost a hand in the battle when Buford was defeated, and probably had known Andrew and his mother when his wound was treated at the Waxhaw church. He now wore a silver knob where his hand had been. That knob came down with a ringing sound when he wanted to make a point in court.

The trials in the courthouse were mostly simple matters. Murray sued Gile for borrowing his horse and injuring it. Elizabeth Lloyd sued William Bridges for cutting down a number of her trees. James Davidson sued Charles McDowell for saying "You are a damned scoundrel, and I can prove it!" Actually Davidson would rather have fought a duel over the matter, but his friends had talked him into trying to settle it in court. More serious cases involved horse stealing, burning a barn, and bigamy.

Justice was still not easy to find in the back country. Folks who could bring their grievances to Salisbury could have a trial. But traveling to the county seat, and finding money to put up at the local tavern while the trial was held, kept many people from trying to get justice. Small villages had no policemen, and criminals had many chances to escape between the day they were caught and the day they reached the prison in Salisbury. For that reason, the court traveled around from one village to another.

On September 26, 1787, Andrew Jackson, "a person of unblemished moral character," was appointed to practice as an attorney. He was twenty. Andrew still kept track of his hero, Colonel William Richardson Davie. In May, Davie had been a delegate to the convention in Philadelphia. A lawyer could do very well in politics, Andy thought, and a small idea took hold in his mind.

Jackson traveled around with a judge and another lawyer, gaining experience in small villages where the local tavern was usually the only place large enough to hold court. The jury usually sat on backless benches—one way of making sure they brought in their verdicts quickly.

Andrew Jackson was at the courthouse in Salisbury one November day when Nancy Jarret saw him there. He stood tall and thin, dressed in a new broadcloth suit and ruffled shirt, his dark red hair pulled back in a queue. A few lawyers still wore powdered hair in the back country, but Andy swore forever he never would. Nancy said his hair was made to lay down smooth, she suspected, "with bear's oil."

"He was full six feet tall and very slender," she reported to her friends, who had not seen him lately. "But graceful. His eyes were handsome . . . a kind of steel blue." No matter how often Nancy talked to him, Andrew had the habit of looking straight into her eyes, his never straying from hers for an instant.

After November, Andrew traveled more with the circuit court. He argued cases clearly and well. His sentences were not filled with legal terms and Latin. Courtroom audiences liked him because they could understand everything he said. When he gave his charge to the jury, made up of simple folk like the people he knew in the Waxhaws, he spoke to them in their own language.

"Do what is *right* between these parties," he said. "That is what the law always means."

Andrew visited his friend John McNairy and met the governor of the state, who was a neighbor. North Carolina supposedly went all the way to the Mississippi River. But the settlers who lived in the far western part of the state had banded together to call themselves the "Western District."

This Western District appealed to Andrew Jackson. Since he had been fourteen and first heard of the mountain men at the Battle of Kings Mountain, he had known they were his kind of people. Now, six years later, he tried to talk John McNairy into going over the mountains with him.

McNairy was not so sure they were *his* kind of men in the Western District. His family had money, and he had a comfortable life where he was. But when Andrew talked of vast areas of empty land beyond the mountains, he could get John excited about it.

"Before long, the Western District will be a state of its own," Andrew told him. "Just like John Sevier and the other mountain men organized their own State of Franklin. We could be there at the very beginning of a new state."

In December of 1787, probably with Governor Martin's help, the legislature of North Carolina declared that the Western District should have its own Supreme Court. John McNairy was one of the judges.

"I'm not going alone," said McNairy to Jackson. "You talked me into this. Now you have to go along to help."

In early April 1788, Andrew and John hurried up a red road into the Blue Ridge Mountains. The State of Franklin had fallen and was now part of North Carolina again. But the Western District still went far beyond the Blue Ridge and the Allegheny Mountains to unknown lands. They would have to hurry if they were to reach the town of Jonesborough in time to open the second quarter session of court.

While they rode, McNairy explained Jackson's duties as public prosecutor, or attorney general.

"Just because the court rules that a man must pay a fine, or repay his neighbor for the barn he burned down, does not mean he's going to do it," said McNairy. "That's where you come in. You have to enforce the law."

Andrew nodded. Sounded like his kind of job all right. Beneath him was a stout mare. He had two pistols and a shiny new rifle. Six law books were in his pack. He had sold his brown velvet pantaloons and ruffled shirts and had packed instead flannel shirts, a deerskin jacket, and heavy boots. With every mile, the high mountain land attracted him more. Some day he would sell the Waxhaw land of his father and buy his land in this new country.

Young Jackson knew he was not the brightest lawyer who ever strode into a courtroom. He never had read all the law books in Macay's or Stokes's offices. He had grave doubts about whether he could have won any legal case in Charleston. But he knew he was well enough prepared for the kind of law Americans were going to need in these rough mountains.

He had just turned twenty-one. His fortune, and some pretty girl, was waiting just around the next bend.

Andrew Jackson: The Man

1788   Duels with lawyer Waightstill Avery. Jackson is one of the first to go down the new road to Nashville, then in western North Carolina. Boards with Mrs. William Donelson and meets her daughter Rachel, unhappy in her marriage to Lewis Robards.

1791   Becomes attorney general of the Mero District. He escorts Rachel Robards to her sister's in Kentucky. Later, learning that Robards is divorcing Rachel, he hurries back. They are married in August in Natchez.

1793   Discovers that Robards had not completed the divorce action.

1794   In January, the divorce now complete, Andrew and Rachel are married again. But Rachel never gets over the shame. In years to come Jackson keeps his pistols ready for anyone who insults her.

1795   Buys property near Nashville, where he later builds The Hermitage.

Tennessee, probably named by Andrew Jackson, becomes the 16th state. Jackson is delegate from Davidson County to Knoxville Convention. Then he is elected Tennessee's first representative to Congress in Philadelphia.

Fills vacated seat in the Senate.

Resigns from the Senate and is appointed a judge of Tennessee Superior Court, giving up his own law practice.

Elected Major-General of Tennessee Militia.

Rachel and Andrew move to their new home, The Hermitage, near Nashville. They have no children of their own. This year, Andrew is asked to be the guardian of the four children of Edward Butler, and the next year, to be guardian to the sons of Colonel Thomas Butler. These children do not live with the Jacksons, but when Rachel's brother, Samuel Donelson, dies, his two sons John ("Jacky") and Andrew Jackson Donelson come to live with them.

Fights a duel with Charles Dickinson because he insulted Rachel. Jackson wounded, but since his gun was "at half cock" and had not fired, he is allowed by the rules of dueling to take one shot at Dickinson. He fires and kills him.

Witness in trial of Aaron Burr, but does not give evidence.

The wife of Rachel's brother, Severn Donelson, has twin sons but is so ill she can nurse only one. Rachel and Andrew legally adopt the other twin, naming him Andrew Jackson, Jr.

1812   War is declared against Great Britain. Asked at what age he intended to stop fighting, Jackson once answered, "In the case of Britain, at age 100." Appointed Major General of U. S. Volunteers by Governor of Tennessee.

1813   Takes his militia to Natchez, Mississippi, on the way to New Orleans. Ordered to disband his men far from home, he refuses. Marches them back to Tennessee. Earns name "Old Hickory." Shot at and wounded by brother of man he quarreled with. Leads volunteers against Creek Indians. When Jackson's men destroy the Indian village of Tallushatchee, one Indian boy, age 3, survives. Jackson adopts little "Lincoyer" and keeps him until the boy dies of consumption about 1827.

1814   Defeats Creek and Cherokee Indians. Takes Northern Florida from the British. Fights British near New Orleans December 23.

1815   Wins Battle of New Orleans January 8.

1818   Fights in Florida.

1819   Rachel and Andrew adopt an orphan relation, Andrew Jackson Hutchings, age 6.

1821   Appointed Military Governor of Florida.

1822   Nominated for presidency.

1823   Refuses appointment as minister to Mexico. Elected to Senate.

1825   Defeated as candidate. Renominated by Tennessee Legislature.

1828 Rachel Jackson dies December 28 and is buried in her garden at The Hermitage.

1829 Inaugurated as 7th President of the United States. His niece, Emily Donelson, goes with him to be hostess at formal White House affairs.

1832 Hurries migration of Indians beyond Mississippi River. Black Hawk War.

1833 Inaugurated for second term as President.

1835 Assassination attempt fails.

1837 Jackson returns to The Hermitage.

1840 Takes part in 25th anniversary celebration of the Battle of New Orleans.

1845 Dies at Nashville, Tennessee, on June 8 and is buried beside Rachel at The Hermitage.

Bibliography

Adams, W. H. Davenport. *Curiosities of Superstition*. London: J. Masters & Co., 1882.

Andrist, Ralph K. *Andrew Jackson: Soldier & Statesman*. New York: American Heritage Publishing Company, Inc., 1963.

Bassett, John Spencer, ed. *Correspondence of Andrew Jackson*, vol. 1. Washington, D.C.: Carnegie Institution of Washington, 1926.

Bosquet, Abraham. *Young Man's Vade Mecum on Dueling*. London, 1790.

Burke's Presidential Families of the U.S.A. London: Burke's Peerage Limited, 1981.

Carroll, B. R., compiler. *Historical Collections of South Carolina*. New York, 1836.

Carruth, Gorton, and Associates, eds. *Encyclopedia of American Facts and Dates*, 5th ed. New York: Thomas Y. Crowell Company, 1970.

Hilton, Suzanne. *We the People: The Way We Were 1783–1793*. Philadelphia: The Westminster Press, 1981.

Holcomb, Brent H., and Elmer O. Parker. *Mecklenburg County N.C. Deed Abstracts 1763–79*. Easley, S.C.: Southern Historical Press, 1979.

James, Marquis. *The Life of Andrew Jackson*. New York: The Bobbs-Merrill Company, 1938.

Johnson, Joseph, M.D. *Traditions and Reminiscences of the Revolution in the South*. Charleston: Walker & James, 1851. (Source of anecdotes about Polk children.)

Lancaster, Bruce, and Richard M. Ketchum, ed. *The American Heritage History of The American Revolution*. New York: Simon & Schuster, Inc., 1958.

Lazenby, Mary Elinor. *Catawba Frontier. 1775–1781: Memories of Pensioners*. Published by compiler, 1950.

Lederer, Richard M., Jr. *Colonial American English*. Essex, Connecticut: A Verbatim Book, 1985.

Maple, Eric. *Superstition and the Superstitious*. New York: A.S. Barnes & Co., 1972.

Miller, John, C., ed. *The Colonial Image*. New York: George Braziller, 1962.

Milling, Chapman J. *Red Carolinians*. Chapel Hill: University of North Carolina Press, 1940.

Morris, Richard B., ed. *Encyclopedia of American History*. New York: Harper & Row, 1976.

Randel, William Pierce. *The American Revolution: Mirror of a People*. Maplewood, N.J.: Hammond Incorporated, 1973.

Rogin, Michael. *Fathers and Children: Andrew Jackson and the Subjugation of the American Indian*. New York: Alfred A. Knopf, Inc., 1975.

Rouse, Parke, Jr. *The Great Wagon Road*. New York: McGraw-Hill Book Company, 1973.

Smith, Sam B., and Harriet Chappell Owsley, eds. *The Papers of Andrew Jackson*. Knoxville: The University of Tennessee Press, 1980.

Speck, Frank G. *Catawba Texts*. New York: Columbia University Press, 1934.

State Records of North Carolina, vol. 21. Goldsboro, N.C.: Nash Bros., 1903.

Tompkins, D. A. *History of Mecklenburg County*, vol. I. Charlotte, N.C.: Observer Printing House, 1903.

Walsh, J. H. *Encyclopedia of Rural Sports*. Philadelphia: Porter and Coates, 1855, 1867.

Wheeler, Richard. *Voices of 1776*. New York: Thomas Y. Crowell Company, 1972.

Also deeds, diaries, maps, journals and daybooks, letters, genealogies.

Index

Ohio, 5; Potomac, 5, 7; Yadkin, 7
Roads: condition of, 40, 44; Post roads, 10; Catawba Path, 9–10; Great Wagon Road, 5–9, 96
Robards, Rachel Donelson, 107–110

Saddlemaking, 86, 95
Schools: Academy (at Charlotte), 25, 26, 52, 95; Cummins's, 52–56, 87; Prince Town (Princeton), 28, 51, 56; Reverend Richardson's at Waxhaw, 24, 27, 30, 32, 49, 63
Sevier, John (Jack), 70, 74, 104
Ships (British fighting), 46–47, 59–61
Slaves, 3, 19, 29, 38, 44, 88, 100
South Carolina: Camden, 68, 70, 78–81; Charles Town (also called Charleston), 4, 10, 17, 21, 23, 27, 32, 37, 39–42, 44–46, 49, 51–52, 57–62, 75–76, 84–93; Cowpens, 21, 47, 76; Fort Mill, 16–17; Fort Moultrie (Sullivan's Island), 44, 46–47, 59–60, 62; Hanging Rock, 67–70; Hobkirk's Hill, 79, 81; King's Mountain, 74, 102; Stono Ferry, 57–58; Sullivan's Island, 44, 46–47, 59–60, 62
Stamp Act, 26. See also Taxes

Stokes, Colonel John, 101, 104
Sumter, Colonel Thomas, 62, 66, 68–70, 73, 75
Superstitions. See Fairies; Witches; Customs
Surveyors, 11, 16–17
Swamp Fox. See Marion, Francis

Tarleton, Lieutenant Colonel Banastre, 61, 63–66, 70, 72, 76
Taxes, 12, 26–27, 37. See also Acts
Tea, 27, 37, 40; Tea Act, 37, 39; Tea parties, 40–41
Tennessee (cities in western North Carolina before 1796): Jonesborough, 104; Knoxville, 108; Nashville, 107, 110
Tories/Loyalists, 37, 39–40, 42, 45, 56–57, 59, 62, 68, 75–79, 83, 87
Tryon, Governor William, 26

Virginia: Roanoke, 7; Yorktown, 85

Wagon trains, 5, 44
Wars: Revolutionary, 23–86; War of 1812, 109; War in Florida, 109; Black Hawk War, 110
Washington, General George, 44, 47, 56, 85
Weddings, 88, 107
Witches, 4